KT-179-668

C015279671

A Viking in the Family

A VIKING IN THE FAMILY

AND OTHER FAMILY TREE TALES

KEITH GREGSON

First published 2011

The History Press
The Mill, Brimscombe Port
Stroud, Gloucestershire, GL5 2QG
www.thehistorypress.co.uk

British Library Cataloguing in Publication Data.
A catalogue record for this book is available from the British Library.

ISBN 978 0 7524 5772 7

Typesetting and origination by The History Press
Production managed by Jellyfish Print Solutions and manufactured in India

CONTENTS

PREFACE

A few months before I began work on this book, I was helping my mother to clear out a garden shed. She was in her late 80s and I had just had my 60th birthday. At the back of the shed was a small two-handled tin tub full of old paintbrushes.

'Do you want to keep this?' I asked.

'Yes,' she replied. 'That was your bath when you were a baby in London.'

I was stunned. When people enquire about my early life, I always tell them how difficult it was for my parents attempting to set up home in post-war London. Both were from outside the capital and had put their savings into a small house. The bathroom and kitchen were combined and with rationing still in force, people had to make do and mend. This bath, purchased at the corner hardware store, was part of that economy. It was either that or the kitchen sink. In all honesty, if I had been doing a more general clear-out without my mother present, the 'bath' would have gone. Now there is no chance. Too big to fit in the family scrapbook, perhaps, but indispensable nevertheless.

Soon after starting work on this book, I was helping her with another sort-out. This time we were looking through the bookshelves in her spare bedroom. Her eyes suddenly lit upon a battered old book entitled *A Century of Creepy Stories*.

'That's the book which brought your dad and I together,' she said.

It is rather a large book and I realised that I had seen it lying around the house for years without having a clue as to its significance. Apparently my mother and father had been in the same friendship group prior to the Second World War and my father loaned my mother this book as he thought she might enjoy it. The war came and both went off to join the forces. When demobbed, they met by accident in 1946. After a brief conversation, mum remembered that she still had the borrowed book and they agreed to meet again so she could return it. So there is no way that *A Century of Creepy Stories* will find its way to a charity shop or, tattered as it is, into the dustbin.

Interesting family stories tend to reveal themselves gradually, often through a chance encounter or discovery. I was 60 when I discovered these two important pieces of information relative to our family.

This book brings together many similar cases of unexpected discoveries from family historians and from my own extended family. They show how evidence, whether written, pictorial or an unusual object, has been used to shape a family's history. Each entry also tells the story behind the discovery, revealing a range of chance encounters and the detective qualities family historians display. These tales are the very essence of family history and I hope that, after reading what follows, you are inspired to delve further into the hidden corners of your family history. There is plenty of first-class material out there for the family historian and, with a little sleuthing and some luck, ancestral bones can be firmly fleshed out.

The book that brought the author's parents together (both also pictured in wartime uniform). (Author's collection)

INTRODUCTION

Family history has exploded in popularity in recent years. Where once gardening and fishing ruled the roost in terms of favourite hobbies, now genealogy or family history have taken over as the pastime of choice for young and old. To find proof, one has only to look at the crowds of family historians at their daily work in local study centres, or to reference the numerous popular monthly publications dedicated to the subject of family history.

The Gregson family, 1954. (Author's collection)

The author's father in the Western Desert. (Author's collection)

Useful notes jotted down by the author's father (now deceased). (Author's collection)

THOMAS JOSEPH GREATOREX
(UNCLE JOE)
10.3.91 BORN LINGFIELD DORMANSLAND SURREY
10.10.12 MARRIED GERTRUDE (B DAG 14.4) MAT 7/57 DAUGHTER
21.7.80 DIED.
LEFT HODNET SEPT '65 AFTER 32 YRS FOR
ANDOVER RD NEWBURY BERKS — BEFORE 1914
Boy Keeper at Woodhouse Oswestry — Gamekeeper
Champion Gundog Breeder, Field Sales
Specialist and Shooting Instructor. Boy
Keeper with his father at Woodhouse
Oswestry — Keeper at Gynley Hall Welshpool
TREVOR TOWER LLANGOLLEN kept mews
berndean Winchcombe Eyles — see paper
cutting 7th Battn KSW Selwyn Jones
Anglesey O Vara line of Spaniels 1933
to Cloondean Hodnet from Cloondean
Welshpool. Auntie Gert Women's Sect.
of B.R. Legion at Hodnet — Secretary
when founded in 1938 — 12 years
Chairman. Left Sept '65 see cutting+
picture VR 89 on Saddle Bch light
Dragoons 13/18 HUSSARS 3 Tower
St Clark (May Garbutt) — No trace
Started with MISS PRUDENCE after
1914-18 War — she came from

10

One result of this boom in genealogical research has been an outpouring of family history-related books. This one, hopefully, is different. Its aims are twofold: to bring to light unusual family stories which were revealed often by accident, or after a new piece of evidence was found; and to be of assistance to family historians looking to make further progress. In an age where school history has become a subject dedicated as much to 'detective work' as rote learning, the art of spotting similarities and differences in historical research comes high up the agenda. This can be applied to family history, too — where family lines naturally differ from each other, yet at the same time produce similarities worthy of note. Understanding such similarities can be of considerable help to other researchers.

The author playing the whistle. (Author's collection)

The entries in this book are deliberately 'bite-sized' and the book itself is one that can be picked up and put down with ease. Both the 'tale behind the tale' at the end of each entry and the 'how to' section at the back of this book aim to be thought-provoking and helpful.

Readers will meet all sorts of interesting personalities and be introduced to a range of fascinating source materials. Ranging from an eighteenth-century shopping note; through to a photograph of an event that never happened; to a family grave without a body in it. We will travel from a far-flung Shetland Isle down to the bottom of a Cornish copper mine, and across the vast margins of the former British colonies via the USA to Australia and New Zealand.

Time, then, for the journey to begin.

I

A 1718 SHOPPING LIST
by Keith Gregson

'So what?', you may justifiably observe. The diaries and journals of the good and great of our land may well record similar events; and there are instances of such records stretching back to Roman times and to places such as the vicus at Vindolanda, Hadrian's Wall, in the far north of England. What makes this discovery special is that the ancestor was not one of the 'good and great' but an illiterate agricultural worker from Cornwall. This must make the survival of a record of his shopping trip all the more remarkable.

The ancestor was Laurence Hendy – my great-grandfather to the power of eleven. The family's Cornish branch, a quarter of my personal bloodline, moved to Cumberland with the nineteenth-century decline of the metal mines in south-west England. Prior to this they had lived and worked in Devon and Cornwall since the commencement of the most commonly recognised genealogical records. There is a family Bible, details of which helped me to trace the Cornish branch back to the village of St Ewe near St Austell in the late eighteenth century. Civil and parish records confirm the accuracy of the family details written in the front of this Bible; and the excellent local registers of baptisms, marriages and burials further enable the line to be traced right back to the reign of Henry VIII. Laurence Hendy (married in 1692 and fathering children shortly thereafter) was one along this line.

Today, the village of St Ewe is famous for its 'Lost' Gardens of Heligan, developed in the Victorian period by the Tremayne family. The Tremaynes had been members of St Ewe's squire-

archy long before this time, and family records can be found in
Truro Record Office. Particularly interesting is a long run of
journals written by Squire Lewis Tremayne in the early part of
the eighteenth century. These are not diaries dealing with life
at the top table, but day-to-day jottings and accounts relating to
the running of the estate – and, although a mere farm labourer,
Laurence Hendy turns up in these on numerous occasions.
Reading between the lines, these journals reveal he was a head
labourer of sorts – a kind of trusty, or possibly an early example
of what was later to become known as a farm bailiff.

As luck would have it, there was only one Laurence Hendy
in the parish at that time, making certain that my ancestor was
the one appearing regularly on the squire's monthly lists. It is
recorded that he was paid both in money and in kind (i.e. hay
and wheat), and there are also references to rent paid by him to
the squire for a cottage known as Spry's House.

For those with ancestors labelled merely 'farm labourer' or
'farm worker' in parish records, extra details such as these may
be considered a godsend – but the best was yet to come in
tracing Hendy. Tremayne was an inveterate page marker and
used any scrap of paper to hand to mark pages he considered
relevant. As some of these scraps contained writing they were
worth investigating further, and one dated 19 January 1718
really came up trumps:

Janauary [sic] the 19 sent by Larans Hendy for Esq Tremaine
2 loafs of suggar the best sort waid [sic] 7 pound wanting 2
ounces at 1-2 [?]
One lofe [sic] waide 4=10 at 10 [?] – The whole [?] Carry
to [?] 8-11=0
Sent you formerly by your man one punchbowl – 0-2-0 [?]
Recd of Larnso Hendo in full of all all [sic] by me Walter Eva

Clearly Laurence Hendy (twice mentioned in the note) had
been sent to the shop for some sugar, a loaf of bread and a

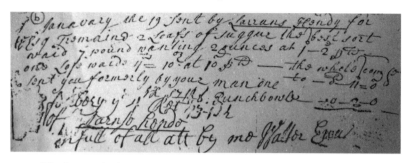

The shopping list from 1718. (Author's collection)

punchbowl. The shopkeeper had merely noted the cost for the benefit of the squire who had sent him.

Thanks to a happy accident, my family now know exactly what one particular, ordinary ancestor was doing on a certain day nearly 300 years ago – a knowledge to which few family historians are privilege.

The Tale behind the Tale

Although Laurence turns up in the family line a long way back, he appears to be the right man as a result of the happy coming together of information from a fairly run-of-the-mill set of genealogical written sources. The starting point was the family Bible cross-referenced into birth, death and marriage certificates; census returns; parish registers; and gravestones in the churchyard at St Ewe. As the parish was a small and tightly knit one, and Cornwall (almost notoriously) toed the line when it came to keeping parochial records, the line back from the Bible to Laurence is also likely to be accurate. (The first person mentioned in the family Bible was born around 1770.)

It is surprising how many journals, diaries and suchlike records *have* survived and can be discovered and consulted in archives around the country. This is especially true of English parishes and it makes the scouring of all records relating to ancestral parishes a worthwhile part of genealogical research – and not just the 'traditional' parish records alone. By chance, another direct male ancestor turned up in the journals, too – David Varcoe, the village carpenter. As overseer of the poor, ratepayer and churchwarden he was also mentioned in other parish records.

It is interesting to note how Latin was still an integral part of the English language in the early eighteenth century. In his note, the shopkeeper uses the Latin ablative term for Laurence's name, *Larnso Hendo*, which means 'by, with or from' Laurence Hendy.

In the twenty-first century shopping trips may still necessitate handwritten shopping lists. Ninety-nine times out of a hundred these will end up in a waste bin. The same must have applied in the eighteenth century, making the survival of Squire Tremayne's list a rarity to treasure.

2

The Lambourn Arsonist

by Dennis Knight

I am now 64 years old and when I was young my mother often spoke of a relative who was hanged for the crime of arson. As is often the case, I didn't take the opportunity to question her about it, and it was only after her death that I discovered a postcard showing a photograph of the gravestone of one John Carter. This postcard is still in my possession and informs me that the gravestone is in the churchyard at Lambourn. The inscription on the stone was as follows:

Here lies the body of John Carter of this Parish, labourer, who in defiance of the laws of god and man wilfully and maliciously set fire in two places to the town of Lamborne on the 19th day of Nov. 1832 and was executed at Reading in the 30th year of his age on the 16th day of March 1833 having desired that his body might be interred here as a warning to his companions and others who may hereafter read this memorial of his untimely end. The wages of sin is death. Repent!

His crime was to set fire to a pub and other buildings in the centre of Lambourn. This resulted not only in the devastation of several buildings, but also in the death of horses in stables, which were burnt at the same time. He apparently did it for no other reason than excitement and was quoted, prior to the fire, as saying: 'I don't think there will be better times at Lambourn till there is a good fire.'

He had been married only a year and was father to two young children. Described as a poorly educated farm labourer, he is also reputed to have been the last man hanged for the crime of arson. Reports of the trial from the *Reading Mercury* and the *Berkshire Chronicle* are lengthy and detailed, with graphic descriptions of the sentence and Carter's reaction to it. These papers also record his reliance on faith and repentance to sustain him, as well as his last meetings with his family. A crowd of 5,000 watched the hanging, which took place on top of the county gaol. Interestingly, one of the papers expressed disgust at the number of females present, which they estimated at two-thirds of the crowd.

The story also has another remarkable twist. Involved in John Carter's crime were three other associates of his who had, in various ways, been complicit in the planning of the fires. Through various ruses, unlike Carter, they had managed to gain acquittals from all charges. However, on the day before the hanging, effigies of these men (Chivers, Winkworth and

Rider) were tied to a horse-drawn cart with the driver dressed as 'Jack Ketch' (the notorious public hangman) and driven to the market place in the centre of Lambourn. Aggrieved villagers carried out a mock trial and found the three guilty alongside John Carter, and the effigies were ceremoniously hanged and burnt. The paper records that the market place was 'crammed' with people.

The Tale behind the Tale

Dennis Knight is a lucky man as it is fashionable to have black sheep in the family. Indeed, many are the members of the Anglo/Scottish border Armstrong and Elliott clans who claim proudly that a number of their ancestors were 'hanged for cattle rustling'. (And then, in the Armstrongs' case, claim that they also produced the first man to walk on the moon and, in George Armstrong Custer, one of the most headstrong daredevils in history.)

Dennis' case study is a fascinating one. Clearly, like many of us, he wishes he had made more use of the memories of family when they were alive. He discovered that the case was a notable one by approaching the history expert at the Reading Local Studies Library. As a result, he was also pointed in the direction of the newspaper accounts of the trial and hanging, as well as details of the mock trial and 'execution' of the other three culprits. More was gleaned through approaching officials at Reading Gaol – a move through which Dennis became aware of a later John Carter and the possibility of yet another notorious criminal in the family. His original contribution goes into much more detail than we are able to publish here.

3

A TRUE GENTLEMAN
by Carol Appleyard

Gibson Kirk was my grandfather. I knew him as Granda Gib. He died a week before I was 10 and I still think of him often with a tear in my eye. He was kind, patient and funny and never had a bad word to say about anyone. He would sit with us on his knees telling stories and jokes, and playing games with us. Some, like 'buzz – knack', he invented for us himself. Here he would wave a brush over the back of our hands and make a buzzing sound. We had to guess when he would stop and get our hands out of the way before the brush hit our hands and 'knacked' – local parlance for 'really hurt'! What I never realised was that my grandfather lived his life in constant pain.

Gibson and his twin sister, Sarah Jane, were born in 1902 – the youngest of nine children. He left school at the age of 14 to take up employment at Hylton Colliery close to the River Wear. At 21, he had to come up from the pit after developing an eye disease common to miners, called Nystagmus. This resulted in uncontrolled eye movements and intolerance to both extreme light and dark, and some colours. This was caused by prolonged work in the dark shafts of the pit.

His daughter Norma also told me that, as a child, he developed recurring pleurisy and was thus prone to problems with his chest. She remembered being asked to wake him up for work. He had a hacking cough and she would watch carefully to see if he was breathing. So severe was the cough that, to her young mind, it could have seen him off at any time. It took Granda two years to recover from the acute stage of this disease.

Eventually he was set to work looking after the bicycle sheds at the pit. Norma recalls taking his 'bait' (lunch box) to him. His little room by the shed was always a whirl of smoke and dust. The floor was layered with fine particles of coal and the big open fire spewed smoke into the air when the draught from the open half-door caught it. Gibson also liked a 'tab' (cigarette) and the combination of all three would make the air 'so thick you could cut it with a knife'. Norma was sure that this contributed to his chest problems.

In time, Gibson was given the opportunity of moving to the pit's medical room and, after training, spent the remainder of his working life as a medical attendant at the pit head. With deteriorating health came extremely painful legs, so much so that his wife Ruth made him light trousers out of sheeting as he couldn't bear the weight of regular trousers on his legs. His colleague, Keith Hall, informed me that he would often go into the medical room to find Granda with his trousers around his ankles and saying: 'Keith, I just canna bear the pain, lad.' At home, according to family members, he would spend time sitting by his coal fire, spitting what came up into its flames.

Granda retired from the colliery in 1967 due to his failing health, and passed away at the local General Hospital in December 1969. His death certificate states that he died of bronchopneumonia and heart problems. As with others who had worked at the pits, no reference was made to his more long-term lung condition.

Keith Hall said he was 'honoured' to have been asked by the family to be a pall-bearer at his funeral, and gave me this description of Gibson that sums him up perfectly: 'He was a true gentleman.'

As a young girl, I didn't know about the pain he suffered in his legs, and as he sat with us on his knees telling stories and jokes, it must have been agony for him. I will always carry in memory his face surrounded by a shock of white hair and the sound of his gentle voice in my ears.

The Tale behind the Tale

Carol Appleyard's sensitive memoir of her grandfather is a lovely piece of writing and something that her family should treasure and pass on. It points to the hardships and poor health resulting from inadequate working conditions. At the same time, she has the courage to add that smoking had not helped the cause and it is noteworthy that Granda Gib's death occurred at a time when reports were starting to point out the dangers of tobacco. The use of the word 'tab' for a cigarette goes back to the early twentieth century and the introduction of a smaller, cheaper brand actually named 'Tabs'.

4

ATTENDING A WEDDING FROM BEYOND THE GRAVE

by Keith Gregson

A giant hand-coloured photograph was discovered at the back of my grandparents' pantry when the house was being cleared after grandmother's death in the 1970s. It was immediately recognised as being taken at great-grandfather's wedding at Barrow in Furness (formerly Lancashire, now part of Cumbria) in the 1890s. 'There's something strange about it', a family member noted at the time. It now hangs in the family home and the mystery has been solved – a mystery that tells us much about the way in which the Victorians looked at life and death.

There are six people in the photograph. The groom, George Gregson (b. 1870 in Preston, Lancashire), is the only one from

The photograph that never was, 1894. (Author's collection)

his side of the family represented. His father had died not long before and his mother many years previously. He had then gone to lodge with the family of his bride, Ann, and was in fact her father's apprentice in the boiler works at the local shipyard. The bride's father is in the photograph, in addition to his other two daughters. The one sitting down was blind as the result of a childhood illness. The lady on the left, looking remarkably ancient for her forty-nine years on earth, is the girls' mother: she had every right to look ill at ease as she had died six months prior to the wedding!

Although those who see the picture eventually note that there is something dramatically wrong with it, this is not self-evident at first glance and the oddities need pointing out. Both the youngest of the girls and their mother are way out of proportion in comparison to the other four in the photograph. If these were their true heights, the 13-year-old youngster would be head and shoulders taller than the rest.

The only daughter of the youngest girl in the photograph knew the full story, and not long after its rediscovery she wrote it down in vivid detail. The picture is, in essence, a composite of three separate photographs. The actual wedding photograph was of the four people on the right of the picture. The two other photographs were earlier individual studio photographs. The youngster's hat has been added on as an afterthought and sits on her head awkwardly like a heavy textbook often used by young Victorian ladies to improve their posture. As the youngster's daughter pointed out, her then 13-year-old mother had not been allowed to attend the wedding as she was still considered to be in mourning for the loss of her own mother.

The youngest in the photograph lived a long and fairly happy life. Not so the others. Both bride and groom died in their 30s – the groom of cancer of the tongue (put down to chain-smoking a pipe) and the bride of organ failure (put down to drink). Drink is said to have seen the end of the bride's father, too – just before his daughter the bride's death. He apparently hit the bottle after losing his job. The daughter Mary, who was blind, was a great trouper. She was active in guiding and taught the piano. She taught my own father to play and he became an excellent honky-tonk pianist. Fiercely independent, she lived on her own and died alone after a fall down the stairs. Her body lay undiscovered for days.

The Tale behind the Tale

'Every picture tells a story' and 'the camera never lies'. These are two tried and tested statements worthy of examination as a result of this study. In the first instance, this picture certainly tells a story but, in hindsight, not the one originally intended. In the second instance, the camera may well snap what is set before it accurately. This can then be manipulated in order to create a falsehood. The cutting and pasting of the deceased onto family photographs may not have been that uncommon in Victorian times.

The origins of both the families portrayed in the photograph are also of interest. The groom's family can be traced back to the cotton mills of Preston and the bride's to the metal manufactories of the Midland Black Country. The development of the steel industry in Barrow in the 1860s was the cause of both their moves, and their stories were easy to put together thanks to a full run of birth, death and marriage certificates and copious census returns. The daughter of the youngster on the photograph also proved an excellent resource with her family tales. The late-born daughter of a late-married lady, she took family stories back an extra generation – with some of her tales stretching back as far as the early nineteenth century. One particularly helpful observation was that her grandfather, the father in the photograph, came north 'to put the Bessemers in' – a wonderfully dateable event. The Bessemer converters, an essential part of the early steel-making process, were established into the Barrow steel works during the early 1870s, making for a perfect fit with other documentary evidence for this particular family.

5

THE VOICE OF MICKEY MOUSE

by Karen Foy

Back in 2003, encouraged by a family friend, I began the task of 'researching my roots'. It wasn't long before I was well and truly hooked.

As a child, Sunday tea times were always accompanied by ten minutes of Disney cartoons. The credits would roll and

Dad would say, 'Watch out for James Macdonald – he's related, you know.' Of course, I watched out for his name but never really questioned who he was.

I have since discovered that John James Macdonald spent a lifetime in movies and music. He was born on 19 May 1906 at the family home in Monks Coppenhall, Cheshire (despite popular belief that he was born in Dundee). His parents were Richard William Macdonald and Minnie Hall – Minnie was sister to my great-grandmother Alice. At the time, two of Minnie's sisters were already in the process of moving overseas so the decision was made to join them. Richard travelled on ahead and by 7 November 1906, Minnie – with baby James, or 'Jimmy', barely 6 months old – had boarded the SS *Haverford* in Liverpool, arriving fifteen days later in Pennsylvania, USA.

As a young man, Jimmy landed a dream job as a musician on the Dollar Steam Ship Lines. In 1934 this led to an opportunity to record music for a Disney cartoon, where he proved himself and secured a coveted permanent position at the Disney Studios. Life was exciting – immersed in the golden era of Hollywood and head of the sound department, Jimmy was responsible for creating thousands of inventions that could produce sound effects for the Disney cartoons and an immense sound library. His contraptions were wild and wacky; he blew through gas lamp chambers to emulate roaring bears and fashioned a note from a harmonica which resembled an arrow hitting its target.

With the sad loss of his mother Minnie earlier in the year, 1946 also marked a significant turning point in Jimmy's career when he was summoned to Walt's office and urged to 'have a go' at the high-pitched voice of Disney's star character, Mickey Mouse. Jimmy was a natural; his first film playing the role was in Mickey and the Beanstalk when Walt raised his salary from £20 to a healthy £50 a week. Jimmy remained the voice of Mickey for over three decades until his retirement in 1977.

Jimmy died on 1 February 1991 aged 85. He is buried at the Forest Lawn Memorial Park in Glendale and takes his rightful place alongside some of the world's most successful entertainers. An inscription on his grave says it all really:

Musician, Actor, Teacher, Friend.
Disney's Sound Effects Wizard and
Second voice of Mickey Mouse from 1946–1977.
Thank You Jimmy.

In 1993, John James 'Jimmy' Macdonald was posthumously named a Disney Legend.

There are many fascinating aspects of family history research, including finding an ancestor with an unusual occupation, a skeleton in the cupboard or a well-hidden secret, but to find someone famous – connected to me – was a real treat.

The Ellis Island website, www.ellisisland.org, proved essential for tracking down my family's entry into the United States, whilst www.ancestry.com helped me to follow their lives once settled via the US census. Www.findgrave.com allowed me to pinpoint Jimmy's final resting place and memorial, and the *Los Angeles Times* shed more light on his working life via his obituaries by searching their archives at http://pqasb.pqarchiver. com/latimes/search.html. For researchers whose ancestors emigrated via the port of Liverpool, there is much to see at the Maritime Museum in the old dock area there, where a large section of the museum is dedicated to the city's maritime links with the New World.

The Tale behind the Tale

Few will have heard of Jimmy Macdonald; yet equally few will not have heard his voice at some time in their lives. Karen Foy has used her detective skills well; she discovered many anecdotes about Jimmy in newspaper obituaries. How nice it is too, to know that future descendants will still be able to hear his voice – and how frustrating it must be to have an ancestor who made a living with his or her voice in the years before recorded sound and left no 'record'. While travelling in the United States recently, BBC television producer Chris Jackson rediscovered recordings of a former master mariner singing sea shanties. These had been made in an Aged Seaman's Home in England during the very early part of the twentieth century. Using the skills of a family historian, Chris found some of the singer's direct descendants. He was able to catch on film their reaction to hearing their ancestor singing. This proved to be a very moving occasion.

6

ADULTERY, INCEST AND SUBTERFUGE

by Jan Llewellyn-Edwards

In what follows, some identifying details have been omitted to protect the sensitivities of the living.

The Fear family bloodline has been traced back to the fifteenth century, when a branch of the family was paying almost half the taxes due in the parish of Chew Magna, in Somerset. Samuel Jacques Fear, a wealthy merchant in Bristol, and his second wife (who was from the same Chew Magna line), had four sons and two daughters. We will follow the fortunes of one of these sons – Jacques Samuel Fear (b. 1844).

Jacques Samuel was admitted to St John's College, Cambridge, in 1867 but does not seem to have graduated.

In 1871 he married Emma Vidal Strickland, the daughter of another wealthy Bristol family, and they had two children together. However, Jacques started an affair with his wife's younger sister, Katherine Jane: it was common knowledge within the family but ignored. Matters came to a head in 1878 when Katherine became pregnant and Emma sued for divorce. The errant couple fled to Tours in France and Jacques did not appear in court to defend the divorce petition.

Jacques was found guilty of adultery and incest in his absence, and the divorce was granted in 1879. Jacques and Katherine stayed in France where their child, also Katherine, or 'Kate', was born in that year. Here the trail went cold, and we simply assumed that Jacques and Katherine had stayed abroad. Then, after an enormous amount of sleuthing, we discovered the truth – and the subterfuge.

Two years after the birth of Kate, the family actually returned to England. At the time of the census in 1881 they were to be found in Bognor, Sussex, living under various assumed names – Langton, Martin, or Langton-Martin. Jacques Samuel Fear was listed as the head of the household but his name was given as J.S. Langton-Martin, and his place of birth as Newcastle 'on' Tyne, Northumberland – when in fact he was born in Bristol.

Their youngest child, Hugh, was the positive link which brought us to uncover this family, and his birth certificate is so much in error that it is worth running through it section by section. His date of birth, '16th March 1881', seems correct; it agrees with the child being recorded as 'under one month' in the 1881 census, and with other information we collected. His birth certificate name, 'John Samuel Langton', was incorrect however; the child had been listed as 'Hugh Samuel Langton' in the 1881 census and he called himself Hugh throughout his life (John being the name of Jacques' first legitimate son). Other family details on the certificate confirm him to have been part of the family I was researching.

Upon his death in Southampton in 1906, Jacques was registered as 'Jacques Samuel L. Martin', but even his death certificate
produced a surprise. E.J. Colston Fear was 'present at the death'
and reported it, declaring he was Jacques' stepbrother; he was,
in fact, his full brother. The brother lived in Bath so must have
travelled to Jacques' deathbed, suggesting the Jacques' had kept
in touch with members of his family throughout.

Is that the end of the story? No – genealogical research
never ends. What happened to Jacques Samuel and Katherine
between 1881 and 1906 still remains a mystery.

The Tale behind the Tale

Tam Llewellyn-Edwards is heavily involved in the research
carried out by the One-Name Society dedicated to the Fear
family, and his cautionary tale should be a lesson to us all. In his
original, lengthier piece, Tam notes that 'we cannot believe all
we read in census returns', and 'it would seem that we cannot
believe all we find on birth certificates either'.

These observations are certainly ones to note when carrying out our own researches. Often we are critical of mistakes
made by transcribers of documents and of the officials who
filled in the registration and census forms, but beware the honesty of the donor of information, too.

There is one instance of a female ancestor who claimed to
be ten years younger than she was for most of her adult life.
Her own mother delivered an inaccurate birthplace to the
numerator for five consecutive census returns, and her correct birthplace was given in 1901 alone. Finally, the subterfuge
passed on another generation and her son wrote down numerous untruths when filling in the 1911 census.

Why did people do this? Jacques Samuel and Katherine
obviously wished to avoid detection and thus be allowed to
lead a quiet life. In the case of the above example and the
1911 census of England and Wales, details may have been inac-

curately given as a generation touched by Edwardian social reforms reflected on the personal cost to them. Government was becoming more bureaucratic and the suspicion was that information being collected would be used to enable the gathering of more taxes. In consequence, some members of the British public decided not to tell 'the truth, the whole truth and nothing but the truth'. In 1911 the head of the household was the more capable of doing this, as, for the first time, he or she had to fill in the form personally. Prior to this, enumerators had collected the relevant information.

7

A Telegram for Admiral Togo

by Keith Gregson

In 2005 the British celebrated the bicentenary of the Battle of Trafalgar and mourned the death of the great naval hero, Admiral Lord Nelson. Across in Japan, the Japanese were recalling the deeds of their own Lord Nelson, Admiral Togo, who a century earlier had virtually wiped out the entire Russian fleet in an encounter at Tshushima. Togo had been trained by the British navy and used some of Nelson's tactics in battle. He also spent much of his career in vessels built at Barrow in Furness and it was during one of his visits to the port there that he encountered another legend in our family – great-uncle Billy.

William 'Billy' Gregson was one of the two sons of George and Ann (featured in the mysterious wedding photograph of

Billy, the family raconteur, *c.* 1914–18. (Author's collection)

Chapter 4). He started his working life as a telegraph boy in the reign of King Edward VII. One day, when the Japanese fleet was paying a courtesy visit to the port, Billy was given a telegram addressed to the great man himself – Admiral Togo of the Imperial Japanese Navy. He duly mounted his bike and pedalled down to Ramsden Dock in Barrow where a Japanese officer in charge of the lighter greeted him.

'Give it to me,' the officer said.

'I can't,' Billy replied. 'Post Office rules say that I must hand it personally to the one named on the telegram.'

Billy was duly ushered onto the lighter and taken out to the flagship lying offshore. Already on board were the mayor and corporation and members of the local press. Billy handed the telegram over to the admiral, according to him 'in front of the clicking cameras of the press'. The journalists even asked for his Post Office cap to be removed and the admiral's hat to be placed on his head. Togo was a cheerful sort and obliged. Billy was then invited to tuck into the mayoral spread, which he did prior to being returned to the dockside in the lighter.

Then things started to take a turn for the worse. The powers that be at the Post Office had expected Billy to hand over the telegram at the dock and head swiftly back. As time passed, somebody was sent to find out what he was up to and discovered only a deserted quayside with an abandoned bike right next to the dock. Fearing the worst, a Post Office representative went to Billy's home to inform his parents that Billy might have fallen into the dock and drowned. When he eventually turned up, neither home nor work was best pleased; he lost a day's pay and got a good telling off from both.

Then there was the time in the First World War when he was filling a bucket of water from the River Somme and a bombardment began. He was forced to spend the next half an hour diving under the surface of the river like a duck hunting for food. After the bombardment ended, he discovered his bucket was riddled with holes and totally useless.

There was also the time in the 1930s when, as an engineer for a cinema chain, he tried to mend a cinema projector only to discover that it was set up for 3D and nobody had told him.

And one of his sons, a boxer at paperweight, used to spar with the legendary heavyweight Brian London in Blackpool in order to improve the heavier man's speed.

Great-uncle Billy – full of tales and anecdotes and a real treasure for the family historian.

The Tale behind the Tale

Every family has its characters, its raconteurs and tellers of tall tales. Are they of any value to the family historian? Of course they are. The context of Billy's Togo tale has been proved historically, although I would query the taking of photographs for the local paper at this stage in history. Togo's visits to Barrow are catalogued in local books and contemporary newspapers but, as yet, the ancestral tale has not been nailed down to one particular visit. Nevertheless, the tales of Admiral Togo, the Somme, early 3D and the boxing are already embedded with the next generation of the family. Such tales are the very stuff of family history and, brought to light controversially by the Alex Haley book and TV series *Roots*, form an element of genealogy difficult to ignore.

8

AN OBSESSION WITH DRINK
by Barbara Pollard (née Swaddle)

My great-grandfather, Mark Swaddle (1848–1917), was obsessed by drink – and strong drink, too – but thankfully not

Mark Swaddle's kindly countenance. (Courtesy of Barbara Pollard *née* Swaddle)

in a way which might initially be imagined. At a very early age he signed the pledge and spent his entire life as an active nonconformist. He also kept journals and notebooks from his early 20s in which he jotted down things of interest to him – things relating to the family, the local community, the region, the country, the world, and, alcohol. In total, these books must contain around 60,000 words and they allow us into the remarkable world that was Victorian England.

Mark spent his working life in the coal-mining industry in north-east England, mostly in charge of the winding engine at F Pit in Washington (formerly County Durham, now part of the City of Sunderland). His father looked after the pit heap, the largest in the county. His brother was in charge of the lamp shed, and at one time the whole family lived in a small terrace just beside the entrance to the colliery.

The journals show us that Mark was dedicated to his work. They are filled with details of events involving pit engines – including breakdowns and explosions. He was also the local representative for the engine men at a time when there was a series of serious strikes and lockouts, and these are covered in

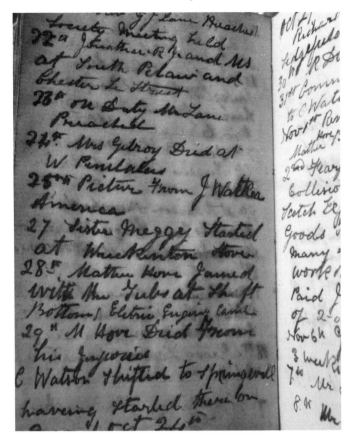

A journal extract highlighting a pit accident. (Courtesy of Barbara Pollard *née* Swaddle)

detail. He was heavily involved in the church Sunday school and Band of Hope. Keen to spend time with his family, he took them to see foreign navies when they were anchored in the River Tyne, and also to fairs and circuses. He noted down when my grandfather was 'breeched' (moved into breeches), and when he got his first bicycle. He recorded local births, deaths and marriages and, above all, he wrote down information on the detrimental effect of strong drink.

In terms of the effect of alcohol, 'Drink did it' was one of his most common comments and he applied it to local men found frozen to death in the snow, at the bottom of coastal cliffs and battered to death in pub brawls. On occasions, when death appeared to be solely through natural causes or old age, he would add the same sombre observation. He had obviously seen the deceased out and about in the community.

There are two large journals: one covers the period from 1867 to the end of Victoria's reign, and the other takes up the story until his death during the First World War. I have one of them and my cousin in Aberdeen has the other. (The first one started life as a kind of account book used by Mark at the pit for noting down the weight of coal tubs.) We are also fortunate in having a number of his effects, including a beautifully inscribed silver-handled walking stick, which was presented to him by his fellow workers. This presentation was reported in the local paper and we have a copy of this article as well as a photograph of him towards the end of his life. This shows him as an upstanding yet kindly man with a twinkle in his eye.

The Tale behind the Tale

Barbara Pollard was born and brought up in Northamptonshire with parents from Tyneside and London. Barbara acknowledges that the survival of the ancestral journals is a fortunate one. Because of the rather macabre nature of some of the content, the journals were considered to be 'unsuitable for the youngsters' in her childhood, and at one point nearly ended up on the fire. Thankfully they were rescued and were later considered interesting enough to feature in a short BBC television documentary.

The Swaddle Journals should be of interest to family historians for a number of reasons. Too often journals and diaries are, in effect, memoirs written so that the writer can be remembered (and in many cases in the way they wish to be remembered). The joy of Swaddle's journals is that they are just general jottings and it is up to the modern reader to work out who he was. He comes out as a sober (naturally) yet far from sombre family man, passionate about his faith and his work – the kind of ancestor many of us would like to have, particularly if the genes were handed down.

During the making of the television programme, Barbara's adult son, also Mark, was interviewed sitting in the driver's chair of the winding engine at F Pit, Washington. He shared his mother's pride in their common ancestry but noted, with the Swaddle twinkle in his eye, that he was 'nothing like his ancestor'.

9

QUITE A SAILOR
by Keith Gregson

My great-grandfather's brother, George Pottinger, was one of the most outstanding merchant sea captains of his age. Born on a tiny island off the main coast of Shetland, he started life as a fisherman and was then recruited to join the merchant navy in South Shields on the River Tyne, in all probability during a sailors' strike in the 1850s. He rose rapidly in the ranks, with his career really taking off when he signed up with the Tyneside firm of Milvain and Company. Here he captained a sailing ship of 727 tons called the *Equator* in which, according to the local *Daily Journal*, he carried out 'several most prosperous voyages'. As the American Civil War broke out, he found himself trapped in the southern port of Pensacola with a freight of cotton. Bravely, he raised the Union Jack and outran the blockading northern warships standing offshore.

George's vessel – a ship in full sail, 1864. (Author's collection)

Records also suggest that George had a reputation for swift Atlantic crossings in this vessel. The *Daily Journal* again notes that he made 'a remarkably fast passage' from the USA to Greenock in 1861. It thus came as no surprise when he was offered command of the full-rigged ship *Ocean Bride*, which features in a number of paintings by contemporary marine artists. He continued to be responsible for some of the swiftest passages on record, making the journey from Quebec to the Downs (between the Kentish town of Deal and the Goodwin Sands) in 1862 in only twenty days.

More significantly, perhaps, George saved the vessel from sinking off the coast of Newfoundland in 1861. The *Ocean Bride* was reported as being 'almost on its beam-ends' with her decks swept with water, yet he managed to bring her back across to Falmouth in Cornwall. The owners of the vessel rewarded him handsomely with 100 guineas and a gold chronometer.

George's story does not have a happy ending, however. On 26 January 1865, the *Ocean Bride* left the Tyne bound for Malaga. George was captain and having problems keeping some of the crew on board. His personal entry in the log, signed when the ship was 'off Shields Bar', indicated that three had deserted and two replacements had been signed up just before departure.

The next entry in the log is not in his hand:

> On the night of the 26th inst. at about 11 p.m., the captain George Pottinger and William Lee, able seaman, were standing on the top galt [sic] forecastle when the ship shipped in a heavy sea, which washed William Lee overboard. He succeeded in saving his life by being entangled in the head and was hauled up in a helpless condition with his collarbone broken. The captain was not afterwards seen and it is supposed to have gone overboard at the same time and been lost.
>
> Signed Magnus Sinclair [first mate]
> William Lee [his mark]

Just a few days later, George's obituary appeared in the local press. The unfortunate 32-year-old was described as 'a most able and successful seaman'. A note of his death at sea was also placed on his young wife's gravestone (she had predeceased him). This is now barely legible but can still be viewed in the old Victorian cemetery at Harton, South Shields.

The Tale behind the Tale

Merchant seamen of the Victorian period left us with magnificent records, which can be studied in various places but mainly at The National Archives at Kew. When they reached the heights of deck officers, records improved, and it is possible to trace the entire career of master mariners and find out more about their vessels by visiting Kew, Greenwich (the National Maritime Museum) and London's Guildhall Library.

George Pottinger (1832–65) has to be recognised as a special case. His many swift passages and deeds of bravery combined to make his loss something worthy of note in the local press.

At the same time, the survival of the relevant ship's log among the samples kept at the National Maritime Museum is a real bonus. If anything can match the thrill of discovering the 1718 shopping list (Chapter 1), it has to be finding the log entry. Reading the last few words my ancestor wrote, before turning the page to find the account of his death in another's hand, was a truly moving experience.

10

A JACK THE RIPPER SUSPECT

by Alison Lawson

It comes as something of a shock when you start out on your family tree and discover you have a renowned murderer in your ancestry.

Frederick Bailey Deeming is on my father's side of the family. His name may not be too familiar to many in the UK but it certainly is to most folk in Australia and, in the global world of modern technology, his name and dastardly deeds are literally 'all over the Internet'.

My ancestor was hanged in Melbourne, Australia, on 23 May 1892 and is described on one website as a 'conman, bigamist and multiple murderer'. He was convicted of the murder of his wife, Emily, whose body had been discovered under the hearthstone of their Melbourne home – but there was more. Soon after Emily's death, a trail was followed back to a previous home in Rainhill near Liverpool, England, which he had inhabited with his first wife and family. When the floor of this house was dug up, the bodies of his other wife, Marie, and their four children were discovered, too.

The Australian murder was big news; the Liverpool murders made it even bigger and it wasn't long before Deeming's name was mentioned in connection with the unsolved Whitechapel murders of Jack the Ripper, which occurred around the same time. In fact, Deeming became known in Australia as 'The Jack the Ripper of the Southern Seas' when rumours began to spread that he had admitted to some of the Ripper murders while in prison.

Frederick Bailey Deeming had first seen the light of day in Ashby-de-la-Zouch in Leicestershire in 1853, but had been raised in Cheshire. He was the youngest of seven and always regarded as strange, being given the nickname 'Mad Fred' when young. His life was littered with petty crimes before he committed the murders, and as he pursued the life of a thief and a confidence trickster he was known to have taken on aliases, sometimes pretending to be a member of the upper classes. His mother was very religious and it was said that he too carried a Bible around with him. When he was eventually arrested in disguise in Perth, Western Australia, after the murder of his second wife, he already had his next victim in mind and was about to marry her.

As you examine the website account of his crimes, you feel that you still cannot rule out the possibility that he may have been Jack the Ripper. The truth is that he was such a slippery character that nobody really knows where he was and what he was up to at the time of the Ripper murders in London. Some say that he was in prison – also that his murders tended to be more organised and calculated than those committed by Jack. Others are not so certain, pointing out that he had been to South Africa at one point and could have been lying low in England at the same time as the South African authorities were chasing him. Another ancestral relative said that he popped in to see them in Liverpool during this period.

Whatever the truth (and we will probably never find out), it is nevertheless a strange ancestry to have to come to terms with.

The Tale behind the Tale

Alison Lawson's tale is one of those salutary ones which might persuade many other researchers to leave the skeleton firmly locked away in the cupboard. It is one thing to be able to say, with a twinkle in the eye, that ancient ancestors had once been pillaging Vikings or ravishing Border Reivers. They operated so long ago that their deeds have become strangely and perversely romantic. In these cases, too, the names of individuals are often not known – merely a simple surname, which in a sense makes all the thieving, roguery and mayhem a little easier to accept. When the errant ancestor lived relatively recently and close enough to have been photographed, does it all then become a different matter? What if somebody in the family bears a strong physical resemblance to the infamous ancestor? Could they or somebody in the family have inherited the errant genes? In any case, it certainly makes for interesting research.

II

TROUBLE WITH RUNAWAYS
by Eileen Hopper

My husband's interesting ancestor was Captain Joseph Scrafton, a Yorkshire-born man who did most of his sailing out on the River Wear. Born in 1833 at Cotherstone in the parish of Romaldkirk, in the 1870s he found himself in charge of the *Mary Ada*, a 329-ton barque built on the river in 1861.

The *Mary Ada* was the first deep-sea vessel belonging to the firm of Horan and Anderson, and Horan himself had

Captain Scrafton, taken on his travels. (Author's collection)

been in charge of the vessel when the first trips were made to the Mediterranean and across to the West Indies. During the captaincy of my husband's ancestor (1871–79), Horan and Anderson communicated with the *Mary Ada* via telegraph and letter – both of which could only be accessed after landing at a port. Much of this correspondence has survived and has been handed down the family – and the contents make for really interesting reading.

If there is one thing clear from these letters, it is that maritime apprentices could be a handful. On one occasion, the writer (either Horan or Anderson) asked for the return of indentures and the account book as an apprentice had run away and they wanted to find him and 'punish him for his conduct'. Another apprentice, named Graham, also ran away and the firm vowed to 'look out for him at this end'. Meanwhile, Joseph was instructed to replace him with an ordinary seaman 'as cheap as you can'. In another instance, a parent's complaint about his son's treatment was pointed out to Scrafton in a letter from Head Office:

> The reason why I write you is respecting your apprentice of which you have two. The father of one of them has been at the office and makes great lamentation about his son and insists that he is ill-used on board of the Mary Ada. As a consequence we defend all our captains and to show that we desire to do the best for the boys and above all things to treat them kindly and well.
>
> Now what I wish to impress upon your mind is that since we are kindly disposed towards the boys, you must be the same as it is in this wise that you will have some satisfaction and benefit from them. Moreover they are only boys and by them you cannot come to much harm in any case. The firmness and kindness I recommend would secure their attachment and good will. As to striking and threatening, it is simply wrong and can be much better done without.

This is a firm yet kindly reprimand – possibly because the master was in reality always the main man, and in the days before good sea–land communication, effectively the one in complete control. As for the captain himself and his character, it is clear that he was much respected and trusted by Horan and Anderson and all the others who employed him. Here is one of a number of references which have survived:

> We hereby certify that Mr. Joseph Scrafton has served us in the capacity of master of the barque Mary Ada for eight or nine years while employed in the West Indies and Mediterranean trades and during this time has been attentive, careful and sober and given us general satisfaction. He leaves our service at this time owing to the sale of the vessel of which he is in command. We believe him to be a trustworthy servant and, as such, we recommend him.

As it happens, Scrafton did not need his reference as he continued to work for Horan and Anderson in charge of a couple of 1,200-ton iron screw steamers – *Effective* and *Resolute*. He eventually moved to a bigger steel screw steamer and ended his days on a Trinity House pension.

The letters and telegraphs make for fascinating reading. They tell us a great deal about Joseph himself but must also be of enormous use to anyone studying life at sea during the era of the sailing ship.

The Tale behind the Tale

The decade from 1870–79 is a particularly interesting one for historians of the sailing vessel. It was during this period that the government introduced the safety load line or 'Plimsoll Line'. Before the bill was passed, safety and security on board ship had been a topic constantly in the newspaper headlines. The general public was becoming increasingly aware of insurance frauds where leaky 'sea coffins' on their last legs were being sent to sea with decks awash, almost in the hope of a profitable sinking. More interestingly, perhaps, the ratepayer was being told of the effect of sea life on the pauper population in seaports. Statistics revealed an ever-increasing number of widows and orphans in receipt of Poor Law relief due to loss of life at sea. Many of these issues were raised in the correspondence received by Captain Scrafton on the *Mary Ada*.

However, the best was yet to come for Eileen Hopper. By a pure quirk of fate, a Leicestershire-based gentleman interested in shipping history made contact on another matter, and a further mass of Captain Scrafton's papers turned out to be in his possession. There are now two large books filled with Scrafton-related material, which give a good all-round overview of life at sea towards the end of the great days of sail.

12

A Hero at Britain's Worst Rail Disaster

by Betty Gregson (née Stephens)

Janet Stephens (*née* Dawson) was my stepmother. She was born in 1895 in the tiny village of Haverigg on the coast of Cumberland. During the First World War she trained as a nurse at Carlisle's Cumberland Infirmary. In May 1915, while still training, she was summoned to the scene of a major railway accident 10 miles to the north of the city. Little did she know that she was about to become involved in Britain's biggest railway tragedy.

Early on 22 May 1915, a local passenger train heading north from Carlisle was parked on one of the main lines near to the signal box at Quintinshill. A troop train heading south from Scotland struck it. The troop train was packed with soldiers of the Royal Scots who were on their way to participate in the Gallipoli campaign, which had just got under way. The wreckage from the crash spilled over onto the other main line where it was struck seconds later by the midnight express on its way from Euston to Glasgow. The resultant 'carnage' saw the death toll rise rapidly from the initial thirty reported in the early editions of the local paper, to 200. The final toll is now put at 227, with 246 people also injured. It remains Britain's worst railway accident.

Hospital staff had been taken to the scene in horse-driven carts and had very little in the way of equipment. When Janet did speak about the disaster, it was of the hopelessness due to the scale of it: 'The casualties were just wandering round or sitting down in the surrounding fields. We had to make do and mend and amputate limbs on the spot to try to save lives. At one point all I had was neat Jeyes Fluid to pour onto wounds.'

Survivors of the great rail tragedy in the surrounding fields. (Author's collection)

THE GREAT RAILWAY DISASTER.

It was on the 22nd of May,
  In the year Nineteen Fifteen,
The great railway catastrophe
  Happened near Gretna Green,
A troop train speeding to the south,
  With the Royal Scots aboard,
Ne'er reached their destination,
  The holocaust—"Oh Lord."

A local to let the express pass,
  Was slipp'd on the main up line,
O, fatal lapse of memory,
  On that Saturday morning fine,
The Signalman, God forgive him,
  To the troop train gave "all clear,"
Into the local train it crashed,
  With a scrunching roaring tear.

From Carlisle, Longtown and Gretna,
  To the rescue many rushed,
They fought like heroes in the flames,
  To save the wounded—crushed,
Amidst the wreckage, groaning,
  They lay in agony,
Each brave heart did his utmost,
  To set the sufferers free.

This terrible disaster
  Shall never be forgot,
All eyes are turned on Quinton's Hill,
  That dread historic spot,
A prayer breath'd on the heroes gone,
  Those gallant soldiers brave,
All Britain gives with many a tear,
  Which waters each quiet silent grave.

HARRY ROBINSON.

A poem about the great rail tragedy. (Author's collection)

Later research into this tragedy has helped us to understand why it was such a disaster, and the outcome of the law case provides helpful clues. The official inquiry laid the blame squarely on two of the railway employees who were in the signal box at the time of the crash; both were eventually imprisoned for manslaughter. Near to the signal box were a couple of siding loops – one on either side of the main lines. Under normal circumstances, the local passenger train would have been shunted onto one of these loops to allow the passage of the major trains along the main line(s). The accidents occurred just after a change in shift. Instructions to prepare for the arrival of the major trains on the main lines were issued but lost in the changeover banter. Both signals remained on 'go' with the local train still standing on one of the main lines.

By the time the first accident had taken place, it was almost too late to prevent the second. The wreckage from the double disaster caught fire and burned through the rest of the day and night. This was because the coaches were mostly made of wood and lit by gas. Intensive investigation subsequently led to the introduction of metal coaches and the abandonment of gas lighting on passenger trains.

Many of the soldiers who survived the crash were fated to die on the sun-drenched cliffs and beaches of Gallipoli or in the trenches of the Western Front. The two railway employees returned to live and work in the local community after serving their prison sentences. As for my stepmother, this was a local incident of national significance, which she was unable to forget.

The Tale behind the Tale

Janet Dawson was married twice. Her first husband was a South African war hero who died of wound complications in the 1920s. She then married a widower and school friend from back home. His wife had died of cancer leaving him with a daughter, and Janet also had a young daughter to look after. For more than forty years, Betty Gregson knew her step-mother as 'mother' and formed a good relationship with her. Which begs the question, should family historians be interested in close relatives who are not 'blood relatives'? An affirmative reply would suggest that we study family history to discover more about ourselves and that we need to know about all those close to us 'in the family' who have had an influence – blood relatives or not.

As a result of Janet's experience at Quintinshill, the family was always interested in the disaster. They built up a small collection of relevant postcards and photographs purchased at jumble sales and from charity shops. One of these contains the handwritten words of a ballad, the first verse and chorus of which puts the tragedy into perspective:

The Gretna Green Disaster – the Tragedy of May
The smashing of the Royal Scots who were upon the way
To reinforce our army and to lick the foreign foe
Where under the leadership of French, our brave lads
     meant to go

Chorus
*They had no thoughts of being smashed while they're upon their
     way*
A few were sad and sorrowful but the many bright and gay
No more upon the Links of Leith these brave Scots lads be seen
For they did meet a sad sore fate down near to Gretna Green.

It is not unusual to find songs, ballads and postcards relating to tragedies across the ages – and many of these tragedies are comparatively small and local. If there is some ancestral involvement then they are worth seeking out.

13

DNA TESTS SHOWING VIKING BLOOD

by Dave Hamm

I wanted to carry out family history research for my father because my paternal grandfather had passed away when dad was only 16 years old. In consequence, he'd never picked up much in the way of family stories and family history.

My dad's folks are mainly from the United States so it was gratifying when, working on the little we knew, we discovered the graves of both his grandfather and great-grandfather in cemeteries on top of the mountains of North Carolina.

From thereinafter it has been a case of one surprise after another, beginning with my grandfather and the information that our family surname was originally spelled with a single 'm'. After another decade of research and delving around, which took me through colonial Virginia and to the probability of English ancestry, I had enough material to co-author a series of relevant books. Unfortunately, due to the loss of records in Virginia, I was not able to trace my line prior to 1750 or to firm up those links with the UK.

It was then that I decided to discover more about my DNA. I signed up for analysis and was amazed to find a number of matches in the UK and a very close match to someone from the English county of Somerset. I was equally surprised to find a significant amount of Viking 'blood' there, too. It would appear that at least one of my ancestors arrived in this area of south-west England during the Norman Conquest. This came

Ancestral gravestones on the North Carolina hilltops. (Courtesy of Dave Hamm)

Ancestral North Carolina. (Courtesy of Dave Hamm)

as quite a shock as, up to that point, one tradition in the States had been that we were of German descent.

Researches carried out since this discovery have led me to Somerset residents with the Ham/m/e surname as early as the middle of the thirteenth century. Moving even further back, I have found out a great deal about the Lords of Ham, important contributors to the history of medieval France.

The Tale behind the Tale

Dave Hamm lives in Ohio in the USA and is now a keen family historian. The way that he became involved in family history research will be of interest to many. How often is it the case that parents or grandparents die young and unexpectedly, and along with them knowledge of the family and its history. For those left behind, the 'need to know' about family history can become all the more urgent as a result of the death. However, DNA testing may well prove a two-edged sword, one of the problems with genealogy being that we have to rely a great deal on ancestors telling the whole truth when answering questions or putting pen to paper. Realistically, there are more cupboards with skeletons in them than we can ever dare to imagine and, in the long run, DNA testing may well present more questions than it actually answers.

On the matter of the Ham family and DNA, Dave further notes: 'on the "I1" DNA haplotype, our HAM DNA Group #1 is about equal to the average (or modal) for this Viking haplotype. We are typically Viking.'

In this context, it is interesting to observe that DNA testing has also been used effectively in the geographic area not far from Dave's 'ancestral home' in England. Here, in Somerset, a group of butchered prisoners of war were discovered by archaeologists in 2009. They had been beheaded, but their DNA pointed to a Scandinavian homeland, and allowed the archaeologists to establish further details about their demise;

the presumption now is that their deaths were at the hands of the victorious and settled Anglo-Saxons.

14

BURIED WITH AN AMPUTATED LEG

by Margaret Weston

Despite years of family tree research, I had no idea that I had an interesting great-great-uncle until I came across a distant cousin in Canada. He mentioned that he had received a letter from a family member who came over to the UK with the Royal Canadian Air Force in 1942. In this letter, the airman noted that he had enjoyed quite a visit to a sleepy place on the borders of the Black Country, which seemed to boast a coal mine every yard or so. Here the airman had searched for information on the Chance family – his ancestors and mine. Serendipity then stepped in as, by sheer 'chance', he met Alfred, the parish clerk of St Mary's Church. Old Alfred (whose name was also Chance) mentioned a rogue in the family – a black sheep who was still fresh in the clerk's memory. It seems this roguish character (since confirmed as my great-great-uncle Joseph Chance) owned a pub or hotel called the Labour in Vain. This hostelry was well known for its pub sign – one which would be considered totally unacceptable today as it showed a black child in a tub being washed by two white ladies.

Old Alfred recalled many tales about Joe but at the time recounted only one: how Joe had lost a leg and supposedly had it buried with his deceased wife until he also died. Apparently, when it came time for Joe to join his leg, the gravediggers dug in vain near his wife until it was found instead by the coffin of a widow of whom Joe had thought more than a little!

Since first learning of this 'interesting ancestor', I have been able to find out more about him. Born in 1805 in a parish in Worcestershire, Joe raised ten children with Ann, his wife, and was a publican. He died in 1874 at Edgbaston where he had gone to live near his daughter, his wife Ann having predeceased him in 1868.

Having heard the original parish clerk's tale, I naturally took an interest in the arrangements in the parish churchyard. Joe and his wife are both buried in Section E, Row I, with a stone indicating their names. What actually became of the amputated leg is a mystery, as is the identity of 'the widow buried nearby'. I have also paid a recent visit to the Labour in Vain.

Sadly, I have been unable to find out much more about the mysterious leg (either the amputated one that was buried or the wooden one worn by Joe). I don't know whether the cause of amputation was an accident or some form of illness or disease. Equally, as I don't know exactly when the leg was removed, I cannot chase up the local newspapers (where an accident, for example, may have been reported).

The Tale behind the Tale

Margaret Weston has been deliberately vague about place names, as she wants to shield some of the correspondents who have assisted her. She does, however, point out that the sign at the Labour in Vain has been changed, although 'there remains a picture of it in the glass in one of the windows'. Her tale also points to one of the great frustrations of family history. Without knowing the exact date of the amputation or the cause, she is not in a position to look at the local newspaper archives. In all probability, this would be a lengthy, thankless and fruitless task.

This tale points to a kind of serendipity which keeps on turning up in family history. Margaret responded to a plea for case studies for this book placed in a family history magazine. Part of the plea consisted of an old family tale of mine, gleaned from a family storyteller who had written down an account of a mysterious Midlands ancestor who had lost his leg in a mining accident but had had it preserved so that it could be buried with him when he died. The setting of my story is the same as Margaret's, and researches carried out since then indicate that this is indeed the same tale, which had been carried down quite distinct lines of the same family. This proves, therefore, that nothing is as likely to survive as a good tale.

15

THE VOICE OF AN ISLAND

by Keith Gregson

Although Walter Williamson (1824–92) was not a blood ancestor, he was a close relative to the direct Shetland branch of my family as three of his children married into it. An ordinary fisherman and crofter on the small island of Burra, Walter has left a mass of evidence relating to his personality, attitudes and beliefs. This is because he represented the people of the small island of Burra when it was visited by a series of officials collecting information for various government reports. Copies of these reports have survived along with verbatim interviews and they tell us a great deal, not only about Walter, but also about the lives of more direct ancestors living in the same small community.

In the middle of the nineteenth century, a Scottish mainland family owned Burra Isle. The fishing and living arrangements

Burra Isle, Shetland. A family croft restored, originally built *c.* 1830. (Author's collection)

for families on the island were organised by a 'tacksman' – a representative of Hay and Company, a fishing group operating out of Lerwick, the island capital. The landowning family had previously organised arrangements such as this, before handing over the task to the tacksman. In 1872 a Royal Commission was sent to Shetland to look into the company's method of financing the fishing and knitting industries. The Burra islanders' main complaint, voiced by Walter, was that they were not allowed to have a shop of their own and couldn't cure their own fish. If they had been able to, they would have been in a position (as he put it) to 'keep the penny amongst themselves' and thus to have lived under less economic pressure. The island shop was owned and run by the fishing company, and 'company stores' was still in operation in Shetland long after being outlawed in England.

As the interview came to a close, the commissioner told Walter that current arrangements could be changed if the enquiry found in favour of the islanders. Walter's response was: 'If we had not been under the belief that it would surely be altered, we would not have come here.'

In 1883 another commission was sent to look into the crofting system and Walter was again on hand to air complaints on behalf of his fellow islanders. These had been gathered together at a public meeting held in the island's church hall. On this occasion, the main objections were to the high rents charged by the landlord and to the lack of reward for tenants who had made improvements to their properties. Walter pointed out he had only been able to afford half a croft: 'The house was hardly worth calling a house. It was nothing at all. The roof was like to come down, so also were the walls.'

He had asked the landlord to improve the property but had been met with a refusal. Deciding to take matters into his own hands, he had extended the length of his property, built up its walls and fixed its roof. The result was a 10s increase in his annual rent. Walter did add, in fairness, that things had generally improved since the previous commission in the 1870s. The islanders were now free to fish and cure, and were better off as a result. However: 'It was only from that time that the Burra Folk had either a stitch of clothes on their backs or a morsel of food.' This last statement is typical of Walter's way with words.

In 1872 he came across as a competent orator, firmly stating the fears of the Burra fishermen but also demanding protection and support from the authorities. Eleven years on, he was even more eloquent: 'Englishmen have the boast of liberty; we could boast of none although we were British men. We were in bondage and slavery, and we had several meetings to get our liberty – the thing desired by all men.' And on the women of Burra: 'The poor women work a good deal harder than many of the rich men's horses. No true gentleman would work his horse so hard as our wives are wrought, and we must needs do that to make a credible living.'

Overall, Walter appeared remarkably fair-minded and realistic:

In Scalloway [Shetland's second biggest community] alone there is not a gentleman or business-man, or fisherman or common labourer, but his father or grandfather was a crofter, and in Lerwick, it has been crofters since it began to rise. The crofters in England, Scotland and Ireland are, I contend, the wealth of the nation. They are there in war and peace, and it is nothing but just and equitable that they should have more fair play when I am dead than they had before, and it is the nation that must do it and not the landlords. Every man is a selfish man, and why not landlords as well as others? We want improvements on our crops, and also on our houses. The blame on it lies on the landlord laws. I don't say it is on the landlords … If I had been a landlord, I am not sure but I should be as bad; but there should be proper laws.

A truly remarkable man, who, through his work with these commissions, has left to us rare evidence of the beliefs and opinions held by ordinary nineteenth-century fishermen and crofters.

The Tale behind the Tale

Royal Commission interviews have survived in abundance and information collected in the lead-up to legislation regarding mines, mills and housing have proved particularly useful to social historians and schoolteachers. The historian Ivy Pinchbeck, for example, used Royal Commission interviews extensively in her magnificent work *Women Workers and the Industrial Revolution 1750–1850* (first published in 1930, with other editions produced in the 1960s and 1990s).

It is sometimes possible to find an ancestor – or someone of around the same age and working in the same mill or mine as an ancestor – being interviewed, and such evidence can really put colour into family tales. There are, however, words of warning! Interviewees were often coached by those in favour of reform, and young mine and mill workers in particular often repeated what they were told to say, making the evidence marginally less valuable. This does not appear to have been the case with Walter Williamson, who was genuinely 'the voice of an island' and, by all accounts, a colourful character.

Other elements of the story make for interesting reading. One of Walter's sons married my maternal great-aunt and emigrated to New Zealand, as did many highlanders and islanders. Two great-uncles signed an 1872 letter of complaint handed over by Walter to the commissioners and, reading between the lines, were actually in the room with him when he was interviewed. According to the records in the final published report, the co-signatories were asked if they had anything to add when Walter had finished speaking. There was no response.

16

NEARLY SHOT BY A VICAR

by Robert 'Bob' Anderson

You won't have to look far for evidence of my ancestor Robert Anderson (1770–1833), the man whose name I share. There is a plaque to him just inside the door of Carlisle Cathedral and a small monument in the cathedral grounds. He was called 'The Cumberland Bard' – and this even though he was a contemporary of the famous Cumbrian-born Wordsworth and other

A study of Robert Anderson. (Author's collection)

well-known Lakeland poets. Robert gained his title because he wrote poems, songs and ballads in the dialect of north Cumberland. During his lifetime many editions of these were published and the songs spread by word of mouth into the local community, turning up in the early twentieth century with the words much changed through time.

Robert was born into a large and poor family in Carlisle, but he was fortunate to receive a fair education at a charity school. He also lived for a short time in London where he became interested in the social entertainment of the time and wrote a number of non-dialect songs. When he returned to Carlisle shortly after 1800, he started to write ballads in the north Cumbrian dialect, with his most fruitful period – judging by those ballads which became most popular – coming between 1802 and 1808.

He painted a world of long dances and cross border dances, like those mentioned in his ballad *The Caldbeck Wedding*:

> The bride would dance 'Cuddle me, Cuddy'
> A threesome then capered Scotch reels
> Peter Weir asked up old Mary Dalton
> Like a cock round a hen next he steals
> John Bell yelped out 'Sowerby Lasses'
> Young Joseph – a long country dance
> He got his new pumps Smithson made him
> And, faith, how he could prance

Robert then went to work at the Calico Printing Works at Carnmoney, near Belfast, where 'Duty soon led me to share my income with the wretched and helpless'. He returned to Carlisle a changed man, but charity on his part gave way to charity of a different sort, being pressed upon him by friends as he 'fell a victim to inebriety'.

His early works continued to be published and republished, but his later material has remained for the most part untouched and little read. Fortunately, many editions of his work survive, a number containing either biographies or autobiographies, of which the most interesting is an autobiography of 1820 which tells of his childhood.

This autobiography makes clear that he had 'many narrow escapes'. On one occasion, 'A clergyman, whom I had respected from my childhood, and would have done any thing to serve him, snapped a pistol at my head, across a small table; without the least provocation'. Luckily, the pistol was not loaded. This was the price he paid for satirical references in his work.

One biography describes the last years of Anderson's life, 'as a sad and mournful chapter … as the fear of ending his days in a workhouse haunted his imagination'. Despite slipping into relative oblivion, Robert has left one interesting heritage. A ballad of his, set to new music by the great song collector of the

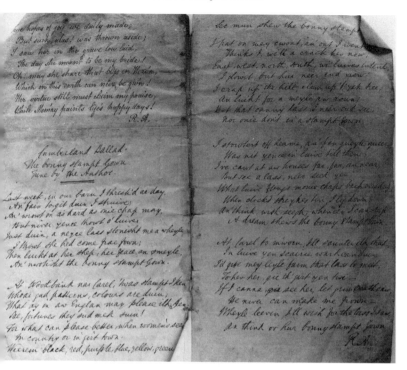

Poems in Anderson's hand. (Author's collection)

late twentieth century, A.L. Lloyd, became a favourite during the folk song revival under the title *The Recruited Collier*. It was even sung in one of the *Sharpe* TV dramas, set appropriately in the Napoleonic Wars of the early 1800s.

The Tale behind the Tale

The 'modern' Robert 'Bob' Anderson lives in the far north of Scotland. Because of his ancestor's writing skills, he is fortunate to have a fairly complete picture of his life. Thousands of us have hand weavers and power-loom weavers in our ancestry and know nothing about them as individuals. In the case of

Robert Anderson (senior) we have a full picture of his doings and movements. The local museum in Carlisle even has on display the flute he used to play, and the library has some of his handwritten manuscripts.

Bob is still trying to follow the Andersons further back and is currently researching the ancestry of Robert's father, Adam. Could the answer lie somewhere in The Cumberland Bard's work? From the tunes the Bard used for his songs it is clear that there were significant links between the family and both the north-east of England and the south of Scotland. Indeed, Robert suspects that the Andersons may be descended from a travelling family because tales have passed down the generations to this effect.

As with all good family histories, the search goes on.

17

A SECRET SECOND
FAMILY IN AUSTRALIA

by Richard Pengelly

It recently emerged that one of my direct (and fairly close) ancestors was something of a dark horse. He was born in England in 1870 and carved out a career in the Royal Navy. When he was in his late 30s, he was seconded to the Australian Royal Navy for a couple of years.

At the time of his secondment to Australia he was already widowed with three children. While 'down under', he fathered a son in Sydney but, unwilling to marry the mother, he skipped ship and returned to Plymouth. Here, he remarried.

Despite his refusal to settle in Australia, he still kept in touch with the Australian mother thanks to the good offices of a couple of former shipmates. One, by then, had become a light-house keeper off the Lizard, while the other was a publican in Plymouth. My ancestor enjoyed a long life and died in 1950.

More recently, the daughter of the Australian 'son' (who, as far as bloodlines go, has the same relationship to the old tar as myself) decided to see if she could make contact with the Pengellys in England and even made trips over here in an attempt to do so.

Ultimately, she sent a letter to our local *Western Morning News*. By a pure stroke of luck, this letter was spotted by my godmother who had just been persuaded to try a free sample of the publication for a week!

As a result, we made contact with our relatives in Australia in the early 1990s and have been in touch ever since.

The Tale behind the Tale

Richard Pengelly's story is one of these wonderful tales that seems to turn up more frequently than one might expect and has, at times, been given as good reason for not delving too deeply into family history! This story also points to the value of contacting modern newspapers close to ancestral homes in the hope of discovering somebody who might add to the family's store of knowledge. Take the case of a researcher who knew that his ancestor had been a gamekeeper on a large estate in Herefordshire in the early twentieth century. From numerous photographs in the family, it was clear that he was quite an imposing character and, according to family tales, on one occasion had been mistaken for King Edward VII while out shooting. The researcher wrote to a number of local newspapers and, despite his appeal coming seventy years after the gamekeeper had been in the Welsh borders, he received a number of replies. One of particular interest came from a gentleman in his 90s who had been a shop boy in the village store where the gamekeeper had been a regular visitor. In a lengthy letter he was even able to recall the ancestor's favourite type of cheese and brand of tobacco. The researcher was able to confirm the accuracy of both these observations, as he knew the gamekeeper as a very old man in the 1940s.

In a similar way, a letter to a local paper enabled another researcher to reunite a 'family heirloom' with its rightful owners. The researcher's ancestor had been saved from drowning in the 1920s and he had bought and inscribed a silver cigarette case to give to his saviour. Unfortunately, he failed to find him again and the case remained with the lucky man's family. Recently, all the tricks of the family historian were employed to track the rescuer and, as luck would have it, he had an unusual name and had lived to a good age on the outskirts of London. An appeal for more information was sent to a local free paper, which was spotted by a friend of the rescuer's family. His wife and son were still alive and the silver cigarette case was duly handed over. The family knew nothing of this deed of bravery as it had taken place before the marriage. Nevertheless, they were overjoyed to have the inscribed memento.

18

HOW A BOER SNIPER JUST MISSED

by Kelsey Thornton

My grandfather, Arthur Rought Brooks (1878–1947), died when I was only 8, but I was always intrigued by a picture of him in his cavalry uniform, and wondered what he'd done in the Boer War. Not long ago my aunt, who is in her 90s, was clearing out her desk. It had belonged to her father who had used it when he had worked as a newspaper editor. In one of the drawers she found an envelope addressed to her father, care of a minister of the church in South Africa. This had been redirected a number of times and finally found my grandfather in the hospital to which he had been sent in 1901. The envelope contained nine photographs which took me back to my youth, and started me off on my current researches.

I discovered first that he'd decided to enlist when he was 21 – inspired, like many others, by romantic patriotism. His 'Short Service Papers' show that initially he joined the 20th Yorkshire Dragoons, but he transferred to a company of the Imperial Yeomanry on news of its formation. This was a mounted regiment and he was a keen horseman.

His 'Description Card for Active Service, to be carried at all times', shows him as Trooper 12187 of the 66th Company of the Yeomanry. Family tradition has it that because of his keenness and skill, he was given a very lively horse, which no other trooper could control. He loved this animal and its temperament, and at every parade he was ordered to gallop at full speed round the parade ground so that the horse was less restless and more controllable when it finally came into line. There were strict orders in the cavalry about the treatment of horses. Well-being, comfort and food were paramount considerations – after all, lives depended upon their fitness. After any exercise, skirmish, or serious engagement, troopers were expected to rub down, water and feed their mounts before they attended to their own needs. This lesson was passed on to my aunt, who always sees to her dogs before she gets her own meal ready.

I also remember his hat, although it is now lost. It had bullet holes in it from his poking his head up when he was part of a guard on an ammunition supply train. At some point during his years of service he received a bullet wound in his right

Arthur Rought Brooks in uniform. (Courtesy of R.K.R. Thornton)

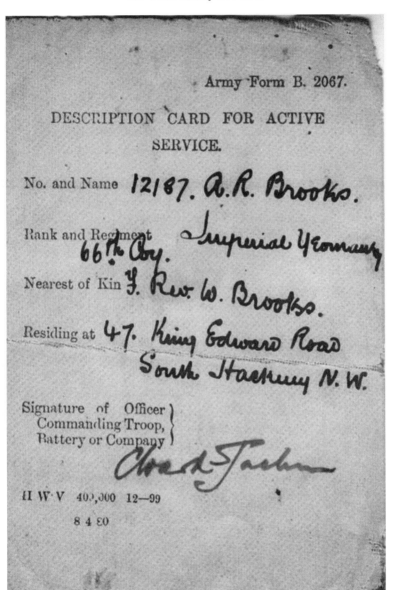

Brooks' army record card. (Courtesy of R.K.R. Thornton)

calf and was taken to hospital. My aunt remembers the wound clearly, as it never healed properly.

Surprisingly, then, his 'Military History Sheet' records 'Nil' in the section headed 'Injuries in or by the Service' – especially as the envelope to which I referred earlier was re-addressed, in the first place to 'The Imperial Yeomanry Hospital, Deelfontein', and later to 'IYH Maitland'. He must have received the letter eventually, as he was able to bring it back home after the war.

My understanding of my grandfather's Boer War experiences was heightened further by the discovery of a piece he published in the *Cambridge Daily News*, which he edited until 1918. He headlined it 'With the Advance Guard. A Day on the High Veldt', and it describes how his troop was ambushed by the Boers:

To our rear and on one side runs a donga, ahead of us a barbed wire fence, skirting a field of maize, through which we intend to ride. Without warning comes a fusilade from the donga and from the maize field – range about fifty yards. There is only one way out, and our officer sees it. 'Right turn – gallop,' he shouts. But the order is unnecessary. With his head low over his horse's neck every man is urging his charger in a wild gallop towards cover about a thousand yards away, while from behind and each side a terrible fire is being poured in. The very horses seem to realise the danger, and with gaping nostrils stretch their limbs and spurn the ground beneath them. There is no question of rank or precedent now; it is a case of the survival of the fittest. In such a moment, I suppose, our thoughts ought to have been solemn; as a matter of fact they were very trivial. I remember distinctly trying to distinguish the sound of the different bullets as they stung by – the b-r-r-r of the Martini-Henry, the sharp hiss of the Mauser, and the ominous crack of the explosive. There is a mad sort of exhilaration, too, as we dash on over anthills, deep ruts, and holes. There is certainly no feeling of fear, merely a curiously detached speculation as to chances of reaching cover without being hit. Our lieutenant pays dearly for his foolhardiness, for he is the first to go down – shot through the whole length of his body. There are two others, and seven horses hit, before we reach safety.

Needless to say, my grandfather survived to tell the tale.

The Tale behind the Tale

Kelsey Thornton's story is a delightful mix of family tale, fortunate discovery and careful research – in the latter case, calling on the same skills he uses in his academic studies as an emeritus professor of English.

The tale of his aunt 'putting the dogs first' at mealtime is also a nice reflection on the influence of her father's military training. Equally, his grandfather's fine account of the Boer ambush may provide us with some hints as to why his grandson eventually enjoyed success in the field of written English.

The story of the 'holey hat' is also a fascinating one and not that uncommon. A work colleague of mine had a similar helmet from the First World War. It had a bullet hole across the very top and belonged to his father who had set himself up as a target by taking the infamous 'third light' for his cigarette. The sniper's rule was first light – see; second light – aim; third light – fire. Older readers may remember elderly men who, back in 'civvie street', still refused to take 'third light' on account of this – including my colleague's father. Also, former sailors would often place a spent match 'upside down' back in the matchbox, a habit gained from the knowledge that dropping it on deck might risk the chance of it reigniting and causing a fire.

One Danish family historian tells of a family Bible with a bullet embedded in it. His ancestor had fought in the Danish

Army, battling the emerging German force in the late nine-teenth century. He had carried the Bible in his breast pocket and it saved his life. It remains a much-valued family heirloom.

19

FROZEN TO DEATH ON THE NORTHUMBRIAN MOORS, PART I

by Anne Roberts

When I was about 5 years old my paternal grandma told me a number of her family tales. She was a native Northumbrian – a cheerful soul who had been widowed in the 1920s and was particularly proud of her links to the border Heron clan. All her tales came in turn from her mother who had been born in Northumberland in 1845.

According to grandma, her own grandmother Eleanor (*née* Arkle, but married into the Heron family) 'had died in a snow-storm out on the Cheviots'. She had lived at Hartside in the Ingram Valley, still a relatively lonely spot today, and one win-ter's day in 1863 'went visiting'. Despite a fierce snowstorm, she decided to make her way home across the moors on foot and never made it. Grandma also told me that a memorial stone marked the place where Eleanor had died and that the last time she was seen alive she had been singing.

When I was still relatively young, my father and I found the grave where Eleanor and her husband John were buried in the churchyard at Whittingham, not far from Hartside, but it was many years later before I had the time to follow the story

Eleanor Heron, who died on the snowbound moors. (Author's collection)

further. There was an account of her death in the regional *Newcastle Daily Journal*, dated Monday 7 December 1863 and headlined: 'SNOW STORMS ON THE CHEVIOTS AND LOSS OF LIFE.' The article mentioned that north Northumberland had just experienced one of its most violent snowstorms ever, and continued:

> We are sorry to state that a poor woman, named Eleanor Heron, wife of John Heron of Hartside, near Ingram, a husbandman, in the service of John William Weallons Esq. perished in the drifts, having a few days previous gone to visit her relations at Rothbury, and was in the act of returning home. She was last seen in life at Alnham, having called on a friend and partaken of some refreshment, and left there about half past 3 o' clock in the afternoon, a distance of about four miles from the place of her residence. The intervening broken footpath passing over a high, wild and

exposed moorland, had no doubt obliged her to succumb to the pitiless storm, as she was found the following morning (Friday) a lifeless corpse on the Chesters farm, about two miles from home by John Hall, shepherd to Mr Chrisp of Prendwick. The deceased was fifty years of age and has left a sorrowing husband and a numerous family to mourn her melancholy fate.

Fifty years after I first heard this tale, I headed across Prendwick Moor in search of the memorial stone. I eventually discovered it lying off the beaten track – a simple stone marked with her name and surrounded by small boulders.

Who put this stone there remains a mystery.

The Tale behind the Tale

What started as merely a family tale recollected from Anne Roberts' youth is now very much a confirmed fact. Religious records, churchyard monuments and newspaper accounts have all been added to the mix, to result in an event that must have been very uplifting – the discovery of the stone itself. A brief account of the family tale was published in a family history magazine in 2008.

As ever, in such cases, intriguing mysteries remain. The family story of the song hints at a strong religious element in the tale. As Anne contacted other members of the Heron clan, it came to be thought that Eleanor had been a member of the Plymouth Brethren and had, in fact, been returning from a 'house meeting' when she died. There was certainly nonconformity in her family, as there was with many families just to the south of the Scottish border, and her baptism was found in congregational records for the community of nearby Harbottle.

Anne's tale confirms at least one interesting observation – that certain families are strongly bonded in family tales. This was particularly brought out in Alex Haley's book and TV series *Roots*, and can be confirmed by members of the Heron Clan worldwide – as can be seen from the next case.

20

FROZEN TO DEATH ON THE NORTHUMBRIAN MOORS, PART II

by Nancy Gill

Eleanor Heron (*née* Arkle) (see Chapter 19) was the sister of my husband's great-great-grandfather Christopher Arkle, who emigrated to New Zealand on the *Chrysolite* in 1861 together with his wife, Margaret Arkle (*née* Bone), and ten of their eleven children. (The eldest, Isabella, remained in England.) They settled in North Canterbury, South Island, where father Christopher and his two sons became farmers. The brothers then moved north of Auckland and established Arkle's Bay.

By a strange quirk of fate we had a family tragedy, too, as Christopher's youngest child, Christiana, perished in a major shipwreck off New Zealand in 1894. Of her we have a family saying, 'born at sea and died at sea', as she was born on the *Chrysolite* on the journey out from England.

Even though she was considered to be a very 'bonny lass', Christiana never married. At age 33 she travelled to Sydney to visit her sister. She boarded SS *Wairarapa* for the journey back to New Zealand and apparently shared her cabin with at least three other young women. Just one day out from Auckland, on the foggy night of 29 October 1894, the *Wairarapa* steamed full speed ahead into the huge cliffs of Great Barrier Island.

Family folklore tells of how, during the night of the wreck, a seaman or steward came along the passage and told the women to follow him to safety. Christiana started out of the cabin but the other three were panic-stricken and she returned to the cabin to encourage them to follow. She could not convince them to leave. Christiana left the cabin just as a wave washed over the ship and down the passageway, washing her and the seaman with it. The man was able to save himself but Christiana and the other three women drowned.

Of the 235 passengers on board, approximately 140 perished. The loss of the SS *Wairarapa* remains the third greatest loss of life on New Zealand waters. Christiana's body was never found, or at least never identified. She is remembered, along with her parents, on a headstone in Addington Cemetery in Christchurch, New Zealand.

Many of the Arkle descendants in New Zealand are keen family historians; we regularly keep in touch with each other and have also established some contacts back in the UK. However, we knew very little about Christopher Arkle's life in his native land, except that his own father had been a Christopher too and at one point he had used the surname Douglas. The story of Eleanor and her death on the Northumbrian moors was new to us in New Zealand and was brought to our attention in a most unusual way (see the Tale behind the Tale).

Eleanor died in the Cheviots. There are a set of hills to the north of Christchurch, i.e. in the North Canterbury district, which are also called the Cheviots, and like their namesake can be snowbound in winter. The New Zealand Arkles, however, settled in a more equitable area to the south of there.

The Tale behind the Tale

Nancy Gibb lives in Christchurch, New Zealand, and is a keen family historian, having researched both her husband's family and her own. The story of how Eleanor Heron (*née* Arkle) died out on the Northumbrian moors became known to her in a 'most unusual way', as she reported to Sarah Warwick, the then editor of the British-based magazine *Family History Monthly*:

> Although not a regular subscriber, I bought the Dec 08 issue of your magazine here in Christchurch New Zealand for something to read over the Christmas holidays. The surname Arkle in Anne Roberts' article 'My ancestor Froze to Death' immediately caught my attention. Eleanor Arkle Heron was the sister of my husband's great-great-grandfather Christopher Arkle.

So it is clear that the story of Eleanor's unfortunate death and the subsequent placing of the marker stone had not passed down the family line in New Zealand. Presumably Christopher was informed of his sister's death, although evidence elsewhere seems to indicate that communication between the growing empire and the UK was not all that it might have been. The family may simply have been unaware of the tragedy.

As to Christopher being the brother of Eleanor, the son of another Christopher and the user of Douglas as a surname, all becomes clear from Eleanor's baptismal entry in the records of the congregational church at Harbottle in Northumberland:

> Ellender [sic] 2nd daughter of <u>Christopher</u> Arkle weaver Sharperton native of Alwinton parish by his wife Elizabeth daughter of John <u>Douglas</u> native of Elderton parish County of Northumberland born 26th March and baptised 29th same month 1813.

Christopher was a far from common Christian name in the middle of the nineteenth century and the Douglases were a well-known border family.

Nancy is now in contact with distant relative Anne Roberts and Anne's own network of family historians, and can swap tales of how an aunt and her niece died tragically at opposite ends of the earth.

21

MAKING QUEEN VICTORIA LAUGH

by 'a family friend'

One of the sayings commonly associated with Queen Victoria is the legendary 'we are not amused'. I, however, know of one occasion when she was so amused that she laughed with delight. The cause of the merriment was two of my relatives.

When they were young, my aunt and uncle lived on the Isle of Wight with their father, who was a photographer and had his own studio in Newport. By 1900, Queen Victoria was an elderly lady living in widowed seclusion in Osborne House, withdrawn from social life and meeting few people. Cared for and attended by the ladies she trusted and tolerated, she occasionally ventured out in her carriage – to the village church or sometimes just for a ride through the quiet country lanes.

Word went around one sunny autumn day that the queen was due to take one of her rare journeys out, and my Uncle Walter, who was 5, and his sister, my Aunt Lily, aged 3, were dressed in their Sunday best and were literally 'stood' outside to watch for the queen's carriage.

My young uncle and aunt sat obediently on the grass verge for some time, until Walter remarked:'When the Queen passes by, I'll take my cap off. That's what gentlemen do.'

Queen Victoria. (Rev. J. Taylor, *The Family History of England*, Vol. I, London, 1890–1910)

Lily considered his statement: 'I'll take off my bonnet then,' she announced.

'No you won't,' her brother retorted. 'Girls and ladies keep their hats on. Don't be silly.'

'I'm not silly,' Lily responded, 'and I'm going to take my bonnet off – so there.'

With this, she gave Walter a slap. Forgetting that he was a 'gentleman', Walter slapped her back and within seconds the pair had become engaged in a bout of fisticuffs. So fierce was the battle that neither of them noticed the approach of the landau pulled by a glossy back horse and bearing the royal coat of arms on the door.

The carriage stopped a few yards away from the combatants and the queen, having spotted the to-do, asked one of the footmen to find out what it was all about. The flushed and disordered youngsters were separated and each told their own side of the story. Their tales were then relayed to the queen who laughed with delight.

This is just one of many of our family tales. On another occasion, my grandfather was invited to Parkhurst Prison to take identity photographs of the prisoners. This was considered something of a novelty at the time. On the way out of the prison, his apprentice dropped all the glass negatives and they were smashed to smithereens.

As to the story of the queen's laughter, my cousin, now in her late 80s, still has a yellowing newspaper account of the incident – it was her mother who was involved in the episode. We suspect that the coachman or one of the servants 'leaked' the story to the local press.

The Tale behind the Tale

Our 'family friend' prefers to remain anonymous for personal reasons, but this is too good a tale to miss. Most families carry a tale or two like this, but the real joy here lies in the proof – the faded piece of newspaper. A tale of equal interest came to light in a Hartlepool classroom in the 1970s when a male pupil brought in another fading piece of newspaper. The article printed on it showed that his direct ancestor had run a pub in the main street in West Hartlepool in Victorian times. Here, the famous professional daredevil Blondin stayed when he came to perform in the town. One of his shows included tying a rope across a street between two chimneys and walking across with a child on his back. During the West Hartlepool performance, that child had been the landlord's son – another of the pupil's direct ancestors. Stories like this are priceless – particularly if they can be backed up by hard evidence such as contemporary news articles.

22

AT HOME IN TRAFALGAR SQUARE

by Eileen Richardson (née Addison)

My direct ancestor, David Addison (1783–1862), lived in Trafalgar Square in the nineteenth century. This Trafalgar Square was not in London but in the ancient parish of Sunderland, not far from the River Wear. Although not as famous as the capital's square, this particular Trafalgar Square still has an interesting history and it was quite an honour to be allowed to live there.

Trafalgar Square was built in the 1840s by a trust and charity with the intention of housing retired mariners who could prove a long connection with the sea and the local port. The trust already had nine houses elsewhere but the new square offered over 100 separate accommodation units, each one capable of housing a man and his wife or a single person, widow or widower. As was the case with the Poor Law system, not everybody in retirement needed accommodation and the same trust also gave support in money or in kind to qualified people living in their own homes.

It was while I was researching this line of the family that I came across not only Trafalgar Square itself, but also the remarkable records kept in relation to folks who had had associations with it over the last 150 years or so. Although the originals are still in the hands of the Trafalgar Square organisation, they have been photocopied and can be consulted on the open shelves in the Local Studies section of our city library.

There are good reasons why these records are extensive. Sunderland was a bustling port filled with people who made a living from the sea, and a room in Trafalgar Square was something to be cherished. The authorities therefore insisted upon proof of strong links with the port, its shipping and trade, and noted down family details in order to avoid fraudulent applications.

My ancestor David appeared twice in the muster rolls for the square – in 1844, when his age was noted as 60, and in 1850 when it was given as 67. On both occasions, his address was given as William Street. In the first case, the scribe wrote that he 'was in the Salisbury Harrison to Quebec and about May 1843 got a serious cold, which brought about dimness of sight'. On this occasion, David was given assistance at home. The later entry states, 'bound to the sea in 1794 and sailed up to 1849 all local vessels – See Case 10 1844 – born September 3 1783'. This time he was offered temporary accommodation in the square.

Although my two family entries were brief, they were really helpful – especially in finding information from the days prior to census and civil registration. I already had evidence of David christened locally: 'the son of David Addison on 3 October 1783'. Learning of his actual birth date exactly a month earlier came as a real bonus. I now know that he went to sea as an apprentice when he was only 11 or 12 and remained there for fifty-five years 'all in Wearside vessels'.

Unfortunately, David didn't put in an application between 1852 and 1855, when a very zealous scribe wrote lengthy tracts on those applying for assistance. Mary Young, for example, had lost her husband, the master of the *Constantinople*. He fell overboard while heading for Callao and belonged to the local parish. Mary was described as being of middle figure with dark hair,

Sunderland's Trafalgar Square. (Author's collection)

grey eyes and a dark complexion. She came from Newcastle originally but was now living in D'Arcy Terrace not far from Trafalgar Square. She was granted an annual pension of £4 8*s*.

Now I am aware of an ancestor at sea during the Napoleonic Wars, I hope I can discover whether he became involved in any major events during the war's famous sea campaigns.

The Tale behind the Tale

The records for merchant seamen are generally good, although this usually applies to the mid-nineteenth century onwards, which would not include most of the period David Addison was at sea. Also, many of the earlier seamen's records in The National Archives are illegible. In cases such as David's, it is often worth looking carefully in local archives for information on maritime activity.

Other ports will also have made arrangements along lines similar to those which led to the construction of Sunderland's Trafalgar Square. An Act of Parliament of 1747 had already allowed for 'the relief and support of maimed and disabled seamen, and the widows and children of such as shall be drowned or slain in the Merchant service'. In order to finance this, sixpence a month was collected from all merchant seamen over 14. Ships' masters were responsible for the collection and for handing the collection over to select customs houses when the ship landed in port.

The centre of Sunderland has moved westwards away from the sea with the passage of time, but Trafalgar Square remains in use, perched on the edge of the original town moor. It is now run by committee and has widened its qualifications for occupancy to include those who worked in the now defunct shipyards.

As to the wars of the late eighteenth century, even if Eileen Richardson's ancestor didn't join the Royal Navy (as a volunteer or pressed man), he may have been close to the action as the merchant navy was often given a supply role. Three years after young David took to the sea, his native town produced its own local and national maritime hero – Jack Crawford. At the Battle of Camperdown in 1797, Crawford famously 'nailed the colours' back to the mast of his admiral's ship, saved the day and provided the English language with a new phrase to describe bold resolution. Young David Addison may have come across Jack at sea or on the streets of the port.

A statue in memory of Jack Crawford, 'the Hero of Camperdown'. (Author's collection)

23

THE PARLIAMENTARY PENSION CON

by Stephen Close

I have an interesting ancestor called John 'Poet' Close. He was born in 1816 in Swaledale, Yorkshire. Even at the relatively early age of 14 he was able to write beautifully and, though trained to be a butcher like his dad, had started printing fly-sheets of his verses to sell at the markets by the time he was 16. He later progressed to writing books. In 1846 he established himself as a printer in Kirkby Stephen in Westmorland, called himself 'Poet' Close and named his house 'Poet's Hall'. His prolific publications included an annual Christmas book; in addition to his verses and stories, these annuals went over the year's events.

In 1858 John married a young widow who had three children, and together they had five of their own. In the summer he lived at Bowness on Windermere in the Lake District, where he had a bookstall at the boat-landing stage on the lake. He also sold his books on railway platforms. At the time of the 1881 census he was living in the main street in Kirkby Stephen. He was with his wife, a son, a daughter and a grandchild, and was described as a 'bookseller and stationer'.

Unfortunately, Poet Close wasn't much of a poet. He was also in the habit of letting his pen run away with his discretion, and in 1859 was taken to court in Liverpool for libel as a result of remarks he had made about a young lady of the Kirkby Stephen district. As a result of the case, he had to pay out £300 in damages.

My ancestor had great difficulty making a living but he benefited from his habit of saying flattering things about

Lord Palmerston. (Rev. J. Taylor, *The Family History of England*, Vol. VI, London, 1890–1910)

those in authority and in high places. This afforded him some position in society and, as a result, through the influence of Lord Lonsdale, Lord Carlisle and other gentlemen, the Prime Minister Lord Palmerston granted him a Civil List Pension in 1860. When it was discovered by Parliament that his writing was far from up to scratch, the pension was stopped and Lord Palmerston gave him £100 from the Royal Bounty in compensation. Poet complained about the injustice of this and continued to write of his 'mistreatment' for the remainder of his life. He died in Kirkby Stephen in 1891.

My ancestor's story is a little sad. He really wanted to be regarded as a Byron or a Burns but ended up being ridiculed. In this context, it is ironic that his work remains sought after and many of his publications now sell for over £100 each.

The Tale behind the Tale

Despite his ancestor's failings, Stephen Close still hopes to have inherited some of Poet Close's genes and has enjoyed some success with his own writing. It is also noteworthy, in terms of Poet's literature, that it is not only the good, great and success-ful who leave a mark.

John was obviously a character and his tireless efforts to better himself mean his descendants have been left with a pretty good all-round picture of the man and his family. There are not many researchers, whose ancestors started out as butchers, who can make this claim. There are useful writings about family and friends composed by John for publication. In addition, portraits of him were painted from a number of different angles and there are handy accounts of his work composed by those less con-vinced by his writing. As historical biographers well know, the ability to collect opposite views of the same person is one to be desired and, in the case of Poet Close, the family has fallen lucky.

24

A MARE CALLED CROW

by Keith Gregson

Catherine Greatorex (d. 1706) was one of my earliest recorded direct relatives living in Alvaston. The place of her birth, baptism and marriage remain unknown, as does her maiden name. I do know she and her husband John raised eight children (four boys and four girls), all baptised at Alvaston. And when Catherine died eleven years after her husband, she was in a position to leave a combined will and inventory which is both full and informative.

Catherine was a tenant of a Sir John Harper, and in her will she asked of him that her second youngest son be allowed to continue the tenancy. She also requested that the youngest son and the youngest girl be permitted to stay there and that the second youngest son should provide them with 'meat, drink and clothes' as long as they worked for him. All three were unmarried and remained so. They died between 1708 and 1710 – all in their early 20s. Four of the remaining five children baptised at Alvaston also received a mention in the will. Three of them received 1*s* each, with the two girls referenced by their married names – Brierley and Archer respectively. Direct ancestor Adam inherited a horse, described by his mother as 'my mare called Crow'. One son, not baptised in the parish, received 1*s*, and there was no reference to the eldest daughter. She may have died or simply fallen out of favour.

The second youngest son was made executor of the will and instructed to divide his mother's property between the three youngest who were to remain in the house – after any debts were paid off. The inventory of the goods she owned, valued at '£19-17-0', is hugely informative. Over half the value of Catherine's property lay in animals: six beasts, twenty-four sheep, three mares and one filly, in addition to the aforementioned 'Crow'. About one-quarter of the value lay in corn and hay, both gathered and still on the ground, plus the farming utensils. The remainder is accounted for by house contents – chairs, stools, brass, pewter, beds, chests and other 'lumber'.

The Tale behind the Tale

The combined will and inventory provide a fine example of a document, which is of use to both the social historian and the family historian. For the social historian, the inventory in particular takes us into the world of the small tenant farmer. If The National Archives' 'historical ready reckoner' is accurate, Catherine's worldly goods, valued at nearly £20 in 1706, would bring in about £1,500 today – a surprisingly small sum for what appears a fair amount of property. These small tenant farmers rose out of the ashes of the feudal system and many of them suffered as a result of the agricultural revolution which came later in the eighteenth century. It thus comes as no surprise to find at least one of her great-grandchildren spending his entire working life as a farm labourer in the nineteenth century.

With so little to go on in terms of written evidence for ordinary folk in the early eighteenth century, the ability to combine a will with a baptismal register is most welcome. The children and their names, and also the married names of two daughters (possibly married outside the parish), are all confirmed, another male child is discovered and one daughter 'goes missing'. Through the inventory, we are welcomed on to a real farm and into a real farmhouse, furnished with chairs, beds and stools and with brass and pewter on the kitchen table and mantelpiece. And then there is the information that two direct ancestors owned a mare called Crow!

Finally, there's the money. Four of the children received the modern equivalent of £4 each – hardly the price of a stiff drink today. And within four years of executing the will, its three main beneficiaries had joined their mother in the village graveyard – and without issue. What then of the family fortune? The search continues.

25

MENTIONED IN MICHAEL FARADAY'S WILL

by Lee Wotton

My great-great-great-great-grandfather Benjamin Vincent (1818–99), of Islington, London, rubbed shoulders with a number of renowned historical characters. He was assistant secretary and keeper of the library at the Royal Institution in London for nearly fifty years and became a close friend to a number of people who researched there. This included the eminent scientist Michael Faraday, famed for his work on electricity and, in particular, dynamos and batteries. Benjamin had free access to Faraday's private quarters within the Royal Institution and their correspondence is well documented and archived. Faraday also provided a surety to enable Benjamin to take the job of keeper of the library at the Royal Institution and mentioned him in his will.

Before becoming a librarian, my ancestor had worked as an editor for a firm of publishers, Gilbert and Rivington. They were responsible for publishing and publicising the eminent scientist's work at what was to prove an exciting time in terms of scientific discovery. Both Benjamin and Faraday were involved with a little-known nonconformist religious group, the Sandemanians. This was a simple faith, which tried to follow the teachings of St Paul and believed in perfect equality of office without any reference to education or position in life. Benjamin joined up in 1832, became a deacon in 1844 and an elder five years later. Faraday also served as an elder.

Prince Albert. (Rev. J. Taylor, *The Family History of England*, Vol. I, London, 1890–1910)

The Sandemanians connected many notable families in London, and its members became well-known scientists, artists, publishers and business founders. Research into these families has led me to look at the formation of the British chemical industry and developments in the newspaper and periodical industry. I also came across the birth of companies such as Barnard silversmiths, publishers Boosey and Hawkes, Newton Patent Agents, and Scientific Instruments and Globe Makers to the queen.

Another regular visitor to the library of the Royal Institution was Prince Albert, who was a great supporter of scientific research and was known to have complimented Benjamin on his work on a number of occasions. A picture of my ancestor can be viewed on the Royal Institution website.

The Tale behind the Tale

Lee Wotton has done a detailed study of Benjamin's correspondence with Faraday and with other members of the Sandemanians. This has led him to his ancestor's old stamping ground – the library at the Royal Institution. The sect insisted upon unanimity in all things – or departure from the 'family'. A tough ask.

The Royal Institution, still famous for its Christmas lectures, has been active since 1791 and its website singles out Lee's ancestor as a historically important member of staff. The 1871 census has him living in London with his family and described as 'assistant secretary and librarian' of the Royal Institution. Intriguingly, one of his daughters is with them, married and named as Sarah Faraday on the same census.

The idea of ancestors rubbing shoulders with the greats is a fascinating one, and the good and great can turn up in strange places. This happened along a minor branch of a friend's family in Victorian times. The sudden death of a male ancestor caused the wife to remarry quickly to protect her two sons and to preserve the family fortune. She wed a close cousin, while at the same time, one of her sons inherited part of a quarry in Wales as part of another will. Her new husband was a solicitor and he and his newly acquired stepson became fascinated by a new invention they wanted to test out in the quarry. The invention was considered too dangerous by others, but the solicitor fought its cause all the way through Parliament and won the day. The name of the invention was dynamite, and the inventor was a little-known Scandinavian called Alfred Nobel.

26

A FATHER'S OLD CLOCK

by Ben Shirvinton

My name is Ben Shirvinton and I am about to sit my GCSE exams at a school in Dalston, Cumbria. People are always misspelling my surname and that is not surprising. When my mother's cousin looked at my dad's family history, she found at least eleven different ways of spelling our name, including Shirvington, Shervington, Sherrinton and Shirrington. She said that this was because of the way people wrote things down in the old days and how my ancestors pronounced their name when they were asked to give it. She also found a will, which my great-great-great-great-grandfather Robert Shervington left when he died in 1854. It is interesting because it mentions his oldest son, David, many times, and David Shirvinton is also my dad's name.

In the will Robert says that when he dies, his wife and all his children (except David) can still live in his house; and when his wife dies, his children (except David) should still be allowed to live there. If they all died then David got the house.

Robert left his wife everything in the house (except his father's clock) and some money to live off. If his wife died, his daughters got all the contents (except his father's clock). One son was left £40, another £20 and one more £5. Three daughters got £20 each and two got £5 each. We had a big family.

By now I was starting to think that poor old David must have done something wrong to be left out, but everything was made clear before the end of the will. Robert had put David in charge of seeing that the money and objects got to the right people and, when he'd finished this, he could keep what was left. What was more important, he also got his father's 'Book'. This was explained to me. Robert had been a joiner so he was really leaving the business to David by handing on his book of work and the names of customers in it. He also left David his father's clock. So that little mystery was solved, too!

There is something else interesting about our family. My name appears on the same family tree as the famous hunter, John Peel. He lived at Caldbeck, just a few miles away from the village of Dalston where I go to school. John was alive in the 1700s and 1800s and a friend of his wrote a song about him. This appears in most books of old English songs and the tune is well known. The first verse and chorus go like this:

> D'ye ken John Peel with his coat so grey
> Do you ken John Peel at the break of the day?
> D'ye ken John Peel when he's far far away
> With his hounds and his horns in the morning.
>   For the sound of his horn brought me from my bed
> And the cry of the hounds has me oft times led
> John Peel's 'view haloo' would awaken the dead
> Or a fox from his lair in the morning.

Although it was a distant cousin of John Peel who married into the Shirvinton family, it is still nice to appear on the same family tree chart as someone so famous.

The Tale behind the Tale

The family tree was prepared especially for Ben Shirvinton by his mother's cousin. Both his mother and the cousin are now deceased so it is nice that he has been left something to work on as he grows older. Often youngsters don't share the enthusiasm of the older generations when it comes to family history, and by the time they do, they have missed out on collecting important evidence. Better, too, if family tales are written down as soon as possible, as when passed down by word of mouth they often become confused and exaggerated.

Ben's point about spelling surnames is also a good one. It is advisable when using the various Internet search engines to try as many variations in spelling as possible. Take, for example, the case of a family with the surname Greatorex. This can appear as Gratrix, Gretrix and Greatrakes, even when the 'Greatorex' form is clearly established in that branch of the family. Although such misspellings are frustrating, they are under-standable. In the early censuses, when Cornish miners were moving around the country in search of work, their accents must have been totally impenetrable, and mishearing and mis-spelling would have been common among the enumerators. Many of us have also come across mistaken transcriptions of both Christian names and surnames made by willing and unpaid volunteers valiantly copying page after page of census and parish register information. This is a thankless task and we ought to be pleased that somebody has given up their time to do it, whatever the errors.

27

THE NAPOLEONIC WAR HERO

by Debbie Kennett

When I began researching my maternal grandmother's Tidbury family, I was intrigued by the unusual choice of Napoleon as a middle name for some of her male ancestors. Could I possibly be connected in some way to the legendary French emperor? As the research progressed, the possibility seemed more and more unlikely. The line went back through a sailor, a royal marine and an unmarried mother to David Tidbury, my great-great-great-grandfather, a humble agricultural labourer who turned out to be not quite so ordinary after all!

David Tidbury was born around 1784 either in Greenham or Newbury in Berkshire. Despite much searching in the local parish registers, I have never been able to find a record of his baptism. He married Phoebe Kewell on 18 March 1822 in East Woodhay, Hampshire. The only unusual aspect of this seemingly unremarkable marriage was that David was around 38 years old – most men at this time married in their 20s. David and Phoebe moved backwards and forwards between Greenham in Berkshire and the nearby parishes of Sydmonton and Ecchinswell just across the county border in Hampshire. In the parish registers and the censuses he is merely recorded as a

David Tidbury's death certificate. (General Register Office)

labourer or an agricultural labourer. He died of 'natural decay' on 19 December 1867, aged 84, in Sydmonton. It therefore came as something of a surprise when I purchased his death certificate and found that instead of being described as an agricultural labourer he was recorded as a Chelsea Pensioner.

With this new angle on my ancestor, suddenly a whole new field of research opened up. His name turned up in the regimental indexes compiled by the specialist Napoleonic War researcher Barbara Chambers. From these I learnt that David had enlisted as a private with the 23rd Regiment of Foot (the Royal Welch Fusiliers) in 1804. Now that I had the name of the regiment I was able to check various records at The National Archives in Kew and the medal rolls to piece together David's remarkable military career. I discovered that he was present at the Battle of Waterloo in 1815, serving in Captain Campbell's No 5 Company. He also participated in most of the key battles and campaigns in the Peninsular War, including Albuera, Badajoz, Salamanca and Vittoria.

The relevant volumes of the 23rd Foot's regimental histories enabled me to trace the movements of the regiment, and consequently David's army career, in great detail. History books provided background information on the conditions the soldiers endured as they marched the length and breadth of Spain, carrying all their heavy equipment and sleeping under canvas only if they were very lucky. The battles were bloody and hard-fought, often with very high casualty rates.

It is quite remarkable that David actually survived his lengthy army career at all, and I can only think that he must have been quite a remarkable character and physically a very strong man. He was finally discharged from the army on 25 May 1821 as being 'unfit for service', and was awarded a pension of 1s (5p) a day. It was now quite clear why he had waited until 1822 to get married. In 1848 David was awarded the Military General Service Medal (MGSM) with eight clasps representing all the battles and campaigns in which he had

David Tidbury's army record. (The National Archives, WO 25/1249, Muster Master Generals' Index of Casualties, 23rd Regiment of Foot, 1st Battalion, 1804 © Crown Copyright)

served. As with all soldiers who were present at Waterloo, he was also awarded the Waterloo Medal in 1816.

The location of David's medals is unknown, but I have been told that it is quite rare to have an MGSM with as many as eight clasps, and especially in combination with a Waterloo medal. Consequently, if the medals ever come up for auction I would have to pay several thousand pounds to reclaim them. The only mystery that remains is why his descendants chose to give their sons the middle name of Napoleon rather than Wellington!

The Tale behind the Tale

Debbie Kennett is a writer on family tree matters and this comes out in the model research she has carried out. Her methods and the material she used for research should be of great assistance to all with military ancestors in the early nineteenth century. Of particular interest is her use of The National Archives at Kew combined with the records of the Royal Hospital at Chelsea (The Chelsea Pensioners). Much of the information here is now available online.

One dilemma I had with this case was giving it a title. 'My ancestor was a Napoleonic war hero' was one possibility, but there is little evidence that anything heroic was actually done. At the same time, 'My ancestor was a Napoleonic war veteran' would seemingly just lump him with the many thousands of men who served at some time during the wars, and he certainly deserves more than that! In fact, simple survival through all those different theatres of war probably justifies the 'heroic' tag and thus the choice is made.

Whatever the outcome of the argument, one thing is certain: anyone who is a fan of Bernard Cornwall's *Sharpe* series – either in its book or television form – would love to have had an ancestor like David Tidbury. It has been said that Sharpe's fictional involvement in so many of the major nineteenth-century conflicts was too good to be true, yet David's war record would seem to prove otherwise. As to the middle name Napoleon, it would seem that the fighting men of Britain had a grudging admiration for the French leader – best seen in the sea shanty *Boney Was A Warrior*, so perhaps the middle name is not all that unexpected after all.

Barbara Chambers' website for British Army (Napoleonic Wars) and Family History Research can be found at http://webspace.mypostoffice.co.uk/~bj.chambers/homepage.html.

28

DROWNED IN THE HOUGLI RIVER

by Barbara Gregson

My mother's great-grandfather, John Cragg (1783–1855), was a successful cabinetmaker and upholsterer in central London, whilst his brother seems to have started life with the East India Company in the early part of the nineteenth century, before moving to India to set up as a merchant. His name, quite distinctive and easy to trace, was Joseph Webbe Cragg (1799–1842). He married in London and had two sons born in India – Cecil Webbe Cragg (b. 1837) and Wallace William Cragg (b. 1840).

Joseph was a prominent member of Anglo/Indian society in Calcutta and it has been possible to trace his activities not only through the usual ancestral sites, but also through popular search engines. These led me to the content of many nineteenth-century journals and magazines that have recently been placed online.

Joseph Webbe Cragg started working life as an employee of the East India Company. *The European Magazine, and London Review* for 1822–23 has him, along with another brother and an older relative, as a purser on board Company ships. His links with the Company are confirmed by a reference to his London wedding in the *Asiatic Journal and Monthly Miscellany*, 1828, which has 'Mr. J W Cragg, late of the Hon. EI Company's service' marrying at St Pancras New Church in London.

By the time of his marriage, Joseph had gone into business in Calcutta and his name appears in numerous different journals in the late 1820s and throughout the 1830s. He was partner in the firm of Bruce, Shand and Company, operating from No 18, Tank Square in Calcutta. Other names that crop up in the partnership are those of William Urquhart, William Bruce, William Patrick, William Shand and Hugh Morton Shand. (The Shands were related to the current Duchess of Cornwall, with one of them a direct ancestor.)

Joseph Cragg seems to have been a leading light in Calcutta society as well as business. He was heavily involved in the Agricultural Society of India and was present at one meeting discussing, among other things, the export of cochineal and tapioca (*Calcutta Monthly Journal and General Register*, 1840). He had a particular interest in tea and chaired a committee of the society which looked at the quality of Assam tea (*Transactions*, 1841). The report itself, dealing with a number of recognisable teas, makes for absorbing reading.

In the *Asiatic Journal*, 1840, he is mentioned as being in support of steamship communication between India and Britain. *The Bengal Directory and Annual Register* for 1838 has him on the committee of an insurance company. Joseph was also involved in freemasonry at a high level and was in the 'eastern chair' of the Lodge of Industry and Perseverance No 109 EC. In addition, he was on one committee for The Bible Society and another for the local Sailors' Society.

The use of Internet search engines has even helped us to plot some of the family's travel arrangements. The *Asiatic Journal* for 1832 has Joseph on board the *Asia* bound for India and China, while *The Calcutta Christian Observer*, 1836, mentions Mr and Mrs J.W. Cragg, merchant, as being on board the vessel *Orient. Parbury's Oriental Herald and Colonial Intelligencer* for 1839 also has details of the travel arrangements of Joseph and his firstborn, Cecil.

In 1842 things started to go wrong for Joseph and the cause, directly or indirectly, appears to have been the 'Opium Wars' between Britain and China. Both the *Law Journal* for the years 1832–49 and *The Rise, Progress and Present Condition of Banking in India*, 1863, tell of economic problems in India due to these wars, and both publications give considerable space to a complex bankruptcy case involving Joseph's firm. By now, however, Joseph was dead and his will (which is in The National Archives at Kew) was being disputed.

The cause of Joseph's death remained something of a mystery until fairly recently. It coincided with problems in his business and obviously led to difficulties as it took the best part of a decade to prove his will. Recently, an old Anglo/Indian journal covering the year of his death was placed online and all became clear: worried by his financial position, Joseph had taken his own life and 'drowned himself in the Hougli River' – a sad end to an otherwise successful life in business.

The Tale behind the Tale

Barbara Gregson's ability to research the remarkable nineteenth-century career of Joseph Webbe Cragg from home can be put down to massive developments in Internet technology. Many old books, journals, newspapers, magazines and documents are now available 'in the original' online and thus can be examined at the press of a button. Equally, the 'Google Books' search engine facility means that there is no need to trawl through page after page looking for a name. The name appears instead already highlighted and with references to other places in the same document where it features.

Using similar research methods, it was possible to find out more about both of Joseph's sons. One served in the army in the Crimean War and was decorated in the Indian Mutiny. His name appears in countless online army records as he remained on the Army List for most of his life. The other son became a solicitor. Their attendance as boys at a boarding school in Brighton was discovered via an online census, and university records can also be accessed via the Internet.

It has always been a recommended practice to urge research-ers to consult original documents as far as possible. So much can become 'lost' and misunderstood in translation and tran-scription. Here it is possible to defer to progress – the items being consulted are effectively original 'copies' of historical documents, and the ability to do that in the comfort of your own home comes as a real bonus.

29

GOOD LOOKS DOWN THE LINE

by Dave Trathen

I was born and brought up in Redruth in Cornwall and am not, strictly speaking, a traditional Tre, Pol or Pen like most Cornish folk – although I have discovered that Trathen is derived from the Tre prefix. The name originated in west Cornwall and means 'a wet sandy patch'. As far as we know there are three Trathen families still around in England, but not related. Ours is based in Redruth, a second is in Hayle (also in Cornwall), and the third one is in north Devon.

Trathen also exists in New Zealand and one of that family branch, Joy, visited my parents in the 1960s when I was just out of my teens. After my parents' deaths I continued the family contact with her, although our blood relationship, if there is one, must be very distant.

Joy Trathen's direct links with the UK appear to have ended in the nineteenth century when a Benjamin Trathen, born at Bere Alston in Devon in 1840, immigrated to Australia. There he married a girl from Camborne – just 3 miles down the road from where I was brought up as a child. Benjamin settled as a sheep farmer in Orange, New South Wales, and died in Australia.

Benjamin and his wife had nine children and the sixth, also Benjamin, moved to New Zealand just after the turn of the century. He had worked in the drapery trade in different parts of Australia before his departure. He married in Nelson at the top end of New Zealand's South Island, and eventually set up a department store which bore the family name. He was a well-known and respected businessman at the time of his death in 1942. This Benjamin fathered five children, including Ellen Joyce, born in 1915, who was known as Joy and was the very lady with whom we were in touch.

In 2004, after my retirement, my wife and I visited Joy at her home in Richmond, which is close to Nelson where her father had his business. I can remember our first encounter vividly. She was in her late 80s and insisted that we visited her – 'before it was too late'. We arrived at the appointed time only to be met at her front door with a stern-faced 'Stand right there!'

Had we offended her even before we entered her house? Not in the least. After a short pause, Joy announced that I was the spitting image of her father at the same age and that she could now go to her grave in the sound knowledge that we were related. Sadly, Joy died in her early 90s shortly after our visit – so we had just made it in time.

But are we really related? In truth, I don't know. My brother is the family historian and he has solemnly announced that his researches are on hold until he is 'unable to play golf' – so I will just have to wait until he is 'totally' retired.

The Tale behind the Tale

Although Dave Trathen is not a student of family history himself, his tale of the meeting is an encouraging one and links nicely with another well-researched 'family reunion' of sorts. After the author Catherine Cookson died in 1998, her biographer Kathleen Jones set out to try and trace Catherine's father. The famous novelist's illegitimacy – the result of 'her mother's love affair with a mysterious handsome stranger' – had inspired much of her fictional writing. In her book *Seeking Catherine Cookson's 'Da'*, Kathleen Jones lays out the trail she followed in her investigation. This book is a tour de force, which ought to be read by all those interested in family history research. In her own researches, Kathleen showed a grit, determination and doggedness which should give hope to anyone pursuing family trails which appear to be going nowhere. No lead was left unfollowed and, in the end, Kathleen was drawn to a house in Whitley Bay and a meeting with two ladies who, if she was correct, were grandchildren of the 'mysterious stranger' who fathered Catherine. As one of the sisters approached, Kathleen 'was amazed to see a Catherine Cookson lookalike coming down the stairs – the face, the eyes, the auburn hair and the lively outgoing manner were uncannily like a younger version of Catherine'. Family photographs plus familiar Christian names and a common congenital disease convinced Kathleen that the family connection was a positive one.

So will Cornish Dave ever firm up the New Zealand line? Joy had a nephew called Benjamin Trathen and traced her tree as far back as another Benjamin Trathen who, according to Dave, married a Mary Dawe in 1774, 'presumably in the UK'. A swift trawl of the usual genealogical sites does not get us much further back, although there appears to be another Trathen branch in Michigan. The answer would seem to lie on (or rather off) the golf course.

30

THE GREAT GRENADIER
by Linda Hall

My great-great-grandfather, Pool Field Davis, was known as The Great Grenadier because he was supposed to be the tallest man in the Grenadier Guards. Born in 1820 to a family of stonemasons and sculptors in Inkberrow, Worcestershire, he joined the Grenadier Guards, married a girl from Kent in 1844 and later went off to fight in the Crimean War.

Pool Davis was supposed to have been a hero, saving the colours at the Battle of Inkerman. An account of his bravery was written up in the *Cassell's Illustrated Family Paper* for Saturday 27 January and also appeared in the *New Zealand Chronicle*. The following extracts from this article tell us a great deal about him:

> Serjeant Davies, the Great Grenadier. – A colour-serjeant of the Grenadier Guards, whose name is P. F. Davies, has been in all the engagements in the Crimea, and has not yet received a wound. He is of herculean frame, and standing six feet four inches high, presents a somewhat prominent mark, and fills a rather large space in the ranks.

And:

> To enumerate the enemy killed and put hors de combat by the single arm of Davies would appear almost incredible; suffice it to say, following the relation of trustworthy witnesses, that he performed prodigies of valour, and gave the Russians a taste of the real metal of which a British Grenadier is composed. Davies has been in the army 17

years, having entered the Grenadier corps as a mere lad of 15; he has, therefore, worked his way up to his present position, and is generally liked by his fellow-soldiers, from the good temper and kindly fooling which he uniformly evinces towards them. In spite of his portly frame and heavy weight, he was capable of running against any man of his regiment, for one hundred yards, and as to jumping, he could, to use the familiar language of his comrades, 'clear a five-barred gate like a swallow'. In all athletic sports, he was a leading authority in the regiment, and took especial delight in seeing the men indulge in them. On landing at Scutari, Davies naturally attracted a great deal of attention. His gigantic size astonished the Turks, and his fine military gait was the general theme of admiration.

A commemorative mug was also issued, using the same picture as the one from the *Cassell's Paper*.

However, the story has a twist to it. Although he fought at Alma, Balaclava and Sebastopol, it would appear that he was sick on board ship and missed Inkerman altogether. A letter came to light exposing him as a fraud and this featured in a Crimean War exhibition at The Army Museum in London a few years ago; I have a newspaper article about the exhibition, which mentions him. The mug was reissued stamped with the name of another soldier who did fight valiantly.

I have found Pool Field Davis in various censuses. In 1861 he was back in Worcester and listed as a stonemason, yet later in the year he turned up as the first drill sergeant at Marlborough College. This is puzzling as although he was tall, he doesn't look that broad, and yet one of the items of the Crimean material refers to him as weighing 25 stones.

In 1865 he was declared bankrupt, so I don't know what went wrong with the job at Marlborough. He then moved to London and was described in the 1881 census as an 'Insurance Agent and Chelsea Pensioner'. He ended up in Bristol, living

The Great Grenadier.
(Courtesy of Mrs Linda
Hall)

near one of his sons, and died there in 1888. He was buried in the Greenbank Cemetery, Eastville, and the story goes that his coffin was so long that it wouldn't go down the stairs of the rather small terraced house; it had to be lowered out of a window. There is also supposed to be a special chair that he had made for him, which is with a distant family member in Ticehurst, Sussex.

The Tale behind the Tale

Linda Hall's fascinating ancestral tale has been put together through the efforts of a worldwide network of researchers interested in 'The Great Grenadier'. She has also used her research into 'GG' – as the family now refers to Pool Field Davis – to draw some interesting conclusions about family names.

'Field' was GG's mother Sarah's maiden name, and it seems to have been a common practice for the eldest child, whether male or female, to be given the mother's maiden name as a middle name. The name 'Pool' baffled me until recently, even though his parents clearly went in for unusual names – he had brothers called Angelo Raphael, Corregio Thomas and Titian Edwin. Sarah Field came from Henley-in-Arden, Warwickshire, and a recently published book on the Warwickshire Hearth Tax Returns of 1670 lists a Mr Pool Field who paid tax on five hearths in Tamworth-in-Arden. He must surely be an ancestor of Sarah's, and I am guessing that his mother's maiden name was Pool.

The story of the grandly named (and grandly framed) Great Grenadier is the very stuff of family history and shows that you cannot believe everything you read, even when it appears in a creditable primary source! There remain positives for researchers into this branch of the Davis family. Although the original tale of his bravery at Inkerman is now discredited, the family has been left with a clear picture of their soldier ancestor. The description given to accompany the tale of his supposed bravery, noting his build, nature and physical prowess, is no doubt accurate and a handy addition to the photographs which have also been handed down.

31

A Nineteenth-Century Cyrano de Bergerac

by Nick Shrewsbury

The fictional Cyrano de Bergerac, as opposed to the real one, is famed for two things – his large nose and his ability to write love poems on behalf of others. My ancestor, Thomas Gregg (1818–79), does not appear to have been famed for his 'proboscis' or 'neb' but he was able to write poetry, and certainly put it to good use with a number of close friends – as my late mum, Joan, discovered in her researches.

The Greggs belonged to the English Lake District. They were farmers, slate miners and copper miners. Thomas himself spent most of his working life at Coniston (then in Lancashire, now part of Cumbria) where he laboured in the copper mines. Towards the end of his life he and his family moved westwards to Millom in Cumberland and the newly prosperous iron mines.

Thomas was a fiercely religious man and preached in a number of nonconformist churches. He was able to put up with the hardships of a miner's existence by looking forward to the afterlife with a mixture of hope and dread. He was a very sensitive man and this comes out in his poetry, as witnessed by an extract from a poem written while 'sheltering from the snow' near the Coniston mine:

> Well, if we have to rhym together
> I'll make a vers about the weather
> The air is cold, the snow decends
> And frost now bites my finger ends
> 　But when the wind turns from the north
> And spring again comes dancing forth
> The sun will shine both warm and clear
> And frost and snow will disappear.

Once in Millom, he found a new set of friends. They had uprooted too – mainly from Devon and Cornwall. Once Thomas' skills with the pen were made known to them, he was swiftly put to work writing little poems to 'send home'. One charming poem, intended for the back of a family photograph, wended its way to grandparents in Devon. The grandfather was blind and Thomas was asked to describe the young grandchildren on the photo in poetic terms. This he did admirably.

The real treasure of the poetry collection, however, is a poem written in 1866 for his friend Thomas Castle, who had moved up from Mary Tavy near Tavistock in Devon. He was simply lost without his girlfriend, Ann Friend, and asked Thomas to inform her of the fact in rhyme:

My time is up I cannot stay
I'm sick of love or fear
For every hour is like a day
And every month a year
   When last I bid my *friend* a due [sic]
Or we shook hands to part
No love ever more more true
Nor had more loveing heart
   By living here so far from thee
I'm near to madness driven
But for to have thee near to me
Would much resembel Heaven.

One of Thomas Gregg's handwritten poems. (Author's collection)

Could I my dearest *friend* embrace
No one on earth should sever
For in my heart she'd find a place
And would be safe for ever
So I will just pack up my cloths
And to my *friend* I'll go
Whose cheeks are like the vergen Rose
And eyes as black as sloes –
Now I'll conclude with ink and pen
For I must leave this place
And turn my footsteps home again
To see thee face to face.

The 1868 marriage of Thomas Castle and Ann Gould Friend is recorded in the Tavistock registration district, which encompassed the village of Mary Tavy. Ann and Thomas were both in their mid-20s and theirs was part of an intriguing double wedding; the other couple was made up of a second Mary Tavy man, Samuel Doidge, who had moved to Millom, and a Cornish lass who had moved there, too. The Doidges returned to Millom to live but the Castles stayed in Devon, and, according to the censuses, raised a family of four children while Thomas Castle found work as a manganese miner.

The Tale behind the Tale

Nick Shrewsbury is Thomas Gregg's great-great-grandson. Born in the UK, Nick is now, like Thomas' brother Ben Gregg, settled in Australia. His mother Joan was an inveterate family historian and Nick has inherited her work post mortem. The family has a Bible belonging to the Greggs and Joan left details of family graves, which are in a prominent place in Coniston churchyard.

As Thomas Gregg spent most of his life in Victoria's reign, his movements were relatively easy to follow via the censuses and records of births, deaths and marriages. The jewel in the crown, however, is the small handwritten book of poems, which has survived. Thankfully many of the poems are preceded by written explanations, enabling the family to find out more about the subjects of the poems which were mostly friends and family. It is thought that one or two poems may have been published in local papers.

32

A PIANO PLAYER IN THE FAMILY

by Janet Thackwray

When I was a youngster in the late 1950s, I was taught how to play the piano and always seemed to have a lot of music to choose from. More recently, when having a general sort-out, I came across a great pile of the music I used to play and realised that it told me a great deal about my family in times past.

The music itself is fascinating – in fact, some of it can be dated back to the middle of the nineteenth century and I have since been informed that the colourful covers alone are of some value. What particularly interested me was that many of them have names scrawled on the cover and, in many cases, a stamp to show where the music was purchased. Naturally, most of the music shops involved were in and around the area where the family lived – Ripon, Harrogate, Leeds and Bradford in Yorkshire.

The oldest sets of music, and perhaps the most intriguing, also have a name on them – Annie Swales. In some cases, the

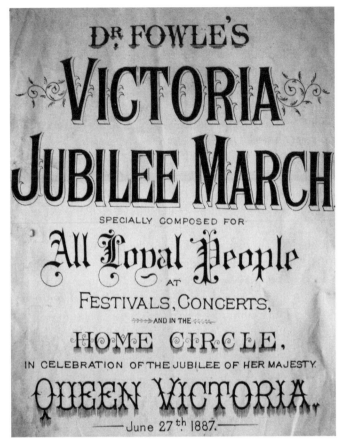

Sheet music from the collection. (Author's collection)

date is on them as well, sometimes handwritten and sometimes put in by the publishers. Annie Swales also put the place
where she was living, Birstwith, on some of the covers. Most
of the music with her name on came from the middle to late
Victorian period.

It is not exactly clear who Annie was or what her relationship with my family was. We are all there in the censuses of

the tiny Hampsthwaite and Birstwith areas – my husband's Thackwrays, my Harper family and the Swales family too, with both a Nancy Swales and an Annie Swales. All were connected to the land in one way or another.

What is certain is that Annie's music was played in our family and falls into three categories: patriotic, classical and popular. Among the patriotic works was the wonderfully titled *Dr Fowle's Victoria Jubilee March Specially composed for All Loyal People at Festivals, Concerts and in the Home Circle in Celebration of the Jubilee of Her Majesty Queen Victoria June 27 1887*. There were also marches linked to successful military campaigns, such as *The Abyssinian Expedition – Descriptive of the Battle and Entry Into Magdala*, *The Defence and Relief of Mafeking* and *March To Pretoria*. The last two are dateable to the Boer War.

The classical collection includes Handel's *Dead March in Saul* (hand-dated November 1901); whilst among the popular songs of the day were *In my Cottage Near The Wood* (with pencilled beat marks throughout), *Home Sweet Home* (no date and purchased at Brandon's Music Dealers, Leeds), *Won't You Buy My Pretty Flowers?* (hand-dated 1901), and *Love Dreams as Sung With Great Success by Grace Stanley*.

Equally interesting are the tutor books. Some of the exercises show the dates when they were practised and the books were obviously passed through the family with a sequence of names crossed out and added.

The family also took a great interest in church affairs and this becomes clear from individual religious songs and general hymn books, collections of religious songs for children, and songs and singing games which were used with the Brownies during the interwar years. We are also good Yorkshire folk so there is a very early copy of the sheet music for *Ilkley Moor Bah tat* in the collection.

An unusual set of sources for family historians, perhaps, but I certainly know a great deal more about one of my ancestors through using them.

The Tale behind the Tale

Imagine what it must be like for a family historian starting from scratch to make such a discovery in a relative's loft! How handy it is also to discover a name, a place and a date close to census time, as in 'Annie Swales, Birstwith, 1901'.

When research was being carried out on a group of English cricketers who competed in the 1900 Olympics in Paris, it was a real boost to know where they were living at that time and the 1901 census proved very useful in this case. From this, it was possible to build up a picture of their families and backgrounds, before moving on to discover other census entries and certificates.

Going back to Janet Thackwray and her music, she also found a collection belonging to another relative from the 1930s and 1940s, and even discovered the family version of *The Teddy Bear's Picnic* which, according to a pencilled note, she had learnt in 1960! We have also discovered an Annie Swales of about the right age marrying into the local Hardcastle family and Janet notes that the Hardcastles owned the farm next to that of her grandparents. Could Annie Swales' music have been passed on as a neighbourly act?

A piano stool packed with Edwardian music was bought from an antique shop in the 1980s. The music was marked with the name of a man called Harold Hunter from Elsecar near Rotherham. Various dates were there showing the collection to have been put together during the late Victorian/early Edwardian period. He had also left a sketchbook full of drawings and paintings in the middle of the collection. From all the information given, it was possible to trace Harold and his family through the censuses.

33

FIGHTING AT THE BATTLE OF TRAFALGAR

by Roger Conway

There has always been a story in our family that an ancestor, John Conway, fought at the Battle of Trafalgar, and that the family has its origins in what is now the Irish Republic. It wasn't until one of my sons married that we had both rumours confirmed as facts. My son's new father-in-law, a keen family historian, picked up the story in conversation and offered to check it out. All of this led to the confirmation that our ancestor, John Conway from County Cork, was on board the *Britannia* during the famous conflict of 1805.

There were two John Conways at Trafalgar; and according to the most complete list of combatants, eleven Conways altogether and all from Ireland. Both Johns served on the *Britannia*. The other John had his roots in County Tyrone in the north of the country. Even if there was a slip somewhere along the line of research, it is clear that my interest in the battle should focus on the *Britannia*. At Trafalgar the ship was under the command of Captain Charles Bullen and, with a hundred guns, was one of the largest ships to take part in the battle. It was on an equal footing with Collingwood's *Royal Sovereign* and Nelson's *Victory* in terms of weaponry, and only the Spanish, fighting on the French side, had a ship that was larger.

At Trafalgar, Nelson attacked in columns, approaching the enemy broadside and in two separate places. The admiral himself told a naval colleague that his intention was to 'surprise' and 'confuse' the enemy and to create a 'pell-mell battle'. The

Victory was at the head of one column and the *Royal Sovereign* at the head of the other. My ancestor's vessel was in sixth position in *Victory*'s column, tucked in between the *Conqueror* and the *Ajax*, both carrying seventy-four guns.

Plans show that the *Britannia* hovered around the edge of the main action for most of the early battle but still had a major role to play. When the front of the French column finally turned to support those affected by the cutting of their line, the *Britannia* and other vessels near her were waiting for them. She grappled with at least one French vessel at close quarters and remained part of a tight little group of British ships which stood firm as guardians until the battle ended in a combination of surrender and retreat.

The *Britannia* was also one of the vessels to take on prisoners and a marine officer on her noted that one prisoner was brought on board dressed as Harlequin. He must have been pressed into the navy after leaving a local theatre.

Although my ancestor seems to have survived the battle, there were a number of deaths recorded on his vessel.

The Tale behind the Tale

For those like Roger Conway who had ancestors, or think they had ancestors, who fought at Trafalgar, the news is all good. The bicentenary of the battle and the equally famed death of Nelson, celebrated in 2005, led to a host of well-researched books and websites dedicated to the battle and the men who fought in it.

Among the books, Tony Barrow's *Trafalgar Geordies and North Country Seamen of Nelson's Navy 1793–1815* stands as a good example of a publication useful to the family historian. The works of historians Roy and Lesley Adkins are also worth visiting. Roy's *Trafalgar – Biography of a Battle* includes information based on a number of eyewitness accounts from among the officers and the ranks. These include midshipman William

Hicks, marine officer Lawrence Halloran and mariner John Nicol.

There is also specific family history material relating to those who fought at Trafalgar. This includes a small pamphlet on finding ancestors in Nelson's Navy in the Federation of Family History Societies pamphlet series, as well as numerous societies and organisations dedicated to Trafalgar ancestral research easily reached via the use of an Internet search engine. The website of The National Archives is also useful. Here the name of a participant in the battle and their basic details can be examined at the push of a button. The National Archives hold many of the ships' logs for vessels which took part in the battle, including the 'Fighting' or 'Saucy Temeraire', famously depicted on its last journey by the artist Turner.

It is worth noting that Trafalgar survivors usually merited a newspaper obituary – especially if they lived to a good age.

34

A COTTAGE FOR LIFE

by Keith Gregson

In an ever-changing and fast-moving world, the tale of Joseph Greatorex (*c.* 1795–1888) is an intriguing one. He spent his entire working life as an agricultural labourer in the Derbyshire village of Alvaston (now a suburb of the city of Derby). Normally, a life like Joseph's may have remained both unremarkable and unobserved, had it not been for one thing. He slept every night of his lengthy life in the same dwelling. Because of Joseph's 'sedentary' nature and his longevity, he was afforded a brief but highly informative obituary in the local *Derbyshire Advertiser and Journal*. This was published on 27 January 1888, six days after his burial and ten days after his death. His age was given as 95 although both census returns and baptismal records have him closer to 93. At the time of his death, Joseph was his village's 'oldest inhabitant', and the author of his obituary noted:

> Had he been an active man of the world, his personal reminiscences taking us back into the last century, would have been interesting and valuable but it so happened that he spent the whole of his long life in the seclusion of his native place, never once sleeping away from the cottage in which he was born.

His parochialism still had benefits for the researcher, however: 'Mr. Greatorex was not only the oldest inhabitant but also a member of one of the oldest families, his descendants claiming for their lineage a continuous residence at Alvaston for the last four hundred years.' The article continues with a description of Joseph's lifelong dwelling – a 'detached cottage' standing 'half way between the Church and the National School, a stone's throw from the yard of the former, where his remains were interred'. Though much changed over the years, the cottage still stands as described opposite the church.

Not only was Joseph's life lengthy, it appears to have been for the most part healthy, as 'he had never known a day's illness until a year or two ago, when the inevitable loss of vitality in the process of time could not be prevented'. This loss of vitality had led to blindness, yet a note of this fact also provides another important piece of family information: 'He had … a good store of purely local knowledge, and when our correspondent had a chat with him, about two years ago, although his eyesight had failed, his faculties were clear enough to enable him to recall and relate many interesting events connected with the parish.'

ALVASTON.

Alvaston has just lost its oldest inhabitant in the person of Mr. Joseph Greatorex who died on the 17th instant, at the patriarchal age of 95 years. Had he been an active man of the world, his personal reminiscences taking us back into the last century, would have been interesting and valuable but it so happened that he spent the whole of his long life in the seclusion of his native place, never once sleeping away from the cottage in which he was born. He had, however, a good store of purely local knowledge, and when our correspondent had a chat with him, about two years ago, although his eyesight had failed, his faculties were clear enough to enable him to recall and relate many interesting events connected with the parish. Mr. Greatorex was not only the oldest inhabitant but a member of one of the oldest families, his descendants claiming for their lineage a continuous residence at Alvaston for the last four hundred years. The detached cottage in which Mr. Greatorex was born, lived nearly a century and died, stands about half way between the Church and the National School, a stone's throw from the yard of the former, where his remains were interred on the 21st inst. He had never known a day's illness until a year or two ago, when the inevitable loss of vitality in the process of time could not be prevented. — *From the Derbyshire Advertiser and Journal, of July 27th,* 1888.

Joseph Greatorex – the rare obituary of an ordinary man, 1888. (Author's collection)

Now a carrot has been dangled. Somewhere in the depths of a late Victorian edition of the *Derbyshire Advertiser and Journal* there may be an article which reveals Joseph's life and deeds in more detail.

Perhaps the key information provided in this obituary is that the family had been in Alvaston 'for the last four hundred years'. The parish records indicate a clear and direct line back to John and Ann Greatorex who were born around 1600. If the 400-year inhabitation is correct, this still leaves another century or more to research, taking the family story back as far as the end of the War of the Roses.

This obituary came into the family as a result of luck rather than good sleuthing. It was discovered in Joseph's great-grandson's desk drawer during a house clearance.

The Tale behind the Tale

The survival and rediscovery of Joseph's obituary has been massively helpful in building up the tree relating to this branch of the family. His parochial life is totally borne out by information gathered from common nineteenth-century genealogical documents. He appears in five consecutive censuses and is described as a farm or agricultural labourer on every one. His age is also fairly consistent (in 1841–45, 1851–56, 1861–65, 1871–76 and 1881–86). His address, however, gives us some pause for thought. Safe in the knowledge that he always occupied the same building, we find it described in three censuses simply as 'Alvaston', in one as 'Elvaston Lane, Alvaston' (Elvaston being a nearby village), and also as 'Back Duck Lane, Alvaston'. Experience elsewhere shows that a change of address doesn't always mean a change of home (especially when it comes to house numbering in industrial towns).

One of the biggest benefits gained from learning of the Greatorexes 400-year residency in Alvaston, is that all the parochial records pertaining to Alvaston are worthy of thorough examination. This has already led to the discovery of an ancient will and to new and surprising information on the relative prosperity of the family in the more distant past (see Chapter 24).

35

HANGED FOR BEING A QUAKER

by John Charlton

Although I live in Canada, I have links to the USA and roots both recent and ancient in England. My interesting ancestor, Mary Dyer, was a housewife whose death by hanging in 1660 helped establish the founding principles of religious freedom and the separation of church and state in America.

Mary is a direct ancestor twelve generations back and, according to my calculations, is one of over 20,000 direct ancestors in my line over this lengthy period. She was born in England as Mary Barrett around 1611 and her marriage to William Dyer/Dier/Dyre is recorded in the church records of St Martin in the Fields, one of London's most central and best-loved churches. The marriage took place in October 1633. A couple of years later, her husband took the freeman's oath in the court in Boston, Massachusetts.

The Dyers were part of the great puritan emigration from England and, by 1637, Mary had become embroiled in controversy. Fellow religious enthusiast Anne Hutchinson was putting forward the theory that God spoke directly to individuals, not through the clergy. This was part of what became known as the Antinomian Heresy, or Controversy, encouraging individuals to self-instruction and Bible-reading as part of worship. Soon after, both the Dyers and the Hutchinsons were banished for their beliefs.

Prior to her departure, Mary had given birth to a stillborn child. The governor, Winthrop, had the body exhumed and a description of it has survived. The governor painted a diabolical picture of the child's body and ensured that all concerned in the colony and back in England were aware of this.

The Dyers settled in Rhode Island and in the 1650s returned to England along with a few friends. Here, Mary came under the influence of George Fox and turned to Quakerism – understandably, as her beliefs and those of the Religious Society of Friends were already close.

Her husband returned to the colony in 1652 but Mary remained in England until 1657, operating as a Quaker preacher. She then returned to America to 'fight her corner' (Quakers were outlawed in the colony). In 1658 she was arrested in New Haven, Connecticut. On release, she went to Massachusetts where she was arrested again, then permanently banned. She returned and was immediately sentenced to death. Her husband's friendship with the governor led to a reprieve.

In 1660 she returned once more to Boston, despite the ban and apparently against the wishes of her husband and family. She was arrested, tried, sentenced to death and hanged on Boston Common on 31 May for the crime of being a Quaker in Massachusetts.

There is a famous painting by an unknown nineteenth-century artist featuring Mary Dyer being led out to execution on Boston Common. A bronze statue of her by Quaker sculptor Sylvia Shaw Judson can also be seen in front of the State Capitol in Boston, and reproductions of the statue are on show at other Quaker centres.

Despite our relationship being distant, I am very proud of my connection with Mary Dyer, and with Anne Hutchinson who played a key role in this story of religious persecution in early colonial America. I think it is a fascinating tale, especially as, ironically, Mary was victimised by Puritans who had themselves fled to America from England in an effort to establish their own community free of religious persecution. Mary's story is almost a parable showing us that if we do not acknowledge history and learn from society's mistakes, we are as likely as not doomed to repeat them.

The Tale behind the Tale

John Charlton is a web designer in Northumberland County, Ontario, Canada. He discovered his ancestor Mary Dyer (*née* Barrett), better known as 'The Quaker Martyr', while corresponding with some of her other descendants on the Internet. As his surname suggests, his more recent roots lie in the lands just south of the Scottish border. John is rightly proud of a direct ancestor who emulated Martin Luther ('Here I stand. I can do no more') by being prepared to pay the ultimate sacrifice for religious belief.

Mary Dyer had strong links with Boston, a city that can be a real gold mine for the family historian. It has an excellent research centre in the city library and a well-staffed genealogical centre a few minutes' walk down the road. Numerous early cemeteries have also survived. Here, monuments constructed from a hard green stone mark graves and, in the vast majority of cases, the names on them are eminently readable. This is true of a number of graves bearing the bodies of those born in England who died in the Boston area in the early and mid-seventeenth century. These gravestones are an interesting contrast to the well-worn and faded sandstone and limestone markers in English churchyards. Nineteenth-century Irish immigration to the city is also well recorded in the cemeteries and archives.

Quakerism is another fascinating research area for the genealogist. In the oldest part of Baltimore, Maryland, for example, a freestanding plaque at Fell's Point honours 'William Fell from Trinkeld, Lancashire' who created the first shipyard there. Trinkeld is a tiny hamlet or farmstead in what was once Lancashire beyond the Sands (now Cumbria). Trinkeld adjoins Swarthmoor, the home of George Fox, the Quaker who married the widow of a distinguished member of the Fell family.

Quakerism was very strong in this area (also known as Furness) and Swarthmoor Hall and its surrounding district remain places of pilgrimage for all those interested in Quaker history.

36

THE ANCHORMAN IN A HUMAN PYRAMID

by Brian Leadley Pollard

My grandfather, who was responsible for my middle name, was called George Leadley Pollard. Leadley is an ancestral surname and the Pollards a fairly well-established family from South Shields (formerly in County Durham). George was one of a large family; his father was called Septimus and he had a brother Septimus, too – a name usually associated with the seventh-born. His father was involved in ship building and repairing and George served his time as a blacksmith. But he also had another 'job': he was the anchorman in a human pyramid, which appeared in shows at the local music hall. This all came about because of his desire to keep fit in his youth. Like many of his contemporaries, he attended the YMCA, which went in for muscular Christianity. Although professional acts travelled around the country to perform, they were usually supported or 'warmed up' by local acts prepared to appear for little money (if indeed any at all).

The act in which my grandfather appeared was typical of this type of support. They would have started the show with a few keep-fit routines and ended their act by building a human pyramid of fifteen young men: five, four, three, two and one on the top. George, as anchor, would have stood in the middle of the bottom five. From first hearing the tale, I imagined that George must have been big and strong. In general, the Pollards were tallish but wiry and muscular. His work as a blacksmith would have seen to the muscularity. As in many physical exercises of this type, technique rather than physical strength must have played an important role.

We think that he performed mostly at a hall known in Victorian times as the Royal Assembly Hall. My sister recalls being told by our father that he visited this theatre to see his own father performing, an indication perhaps that George continued this 'work' after marriage. The theatre later became a popular cinema named the Scala and some parts of the building still stand today. George was also in the Royal Naval Reserve and we have his First World War medals with his number and ERA; RNR stamped on them. The ERA stands for Engine Room Artificer – an ideal position for one trained as a blacksmith.

The Tale behind the Tale

Brian Pollard's tale is a good family one. If told often enough, it is easy to imagine how his grandfather might eventually turn out to have been 'a strong man' working the music halls or even, with the odd slip of the tongue, the circus. In many ways, the real tale is more interesting and gives us a nice insight into the way that the music halls really worked.

George's son (and Brian's father), Wilf Pollard, was a talented cricketer and played for South Shields with and against some of the great West Indian and Indian cricketers of the 1920s and 1930s. (They served as local league professionals.) When a well-known sporting journalist wanted to write a history of the club, he turned to Wilf and interviewed him in detail. The book was well received throughout the cricketing community and remains a wonderful resource not only for students of cricket but also for those interested in Pollard family history. Brian's house proudly parades a number of team photographs featuring his father, some of them now eighty years old.

37

AN HONORARY FREEMAN
OF LONDON

by Barbara Mason (née Flower)

I remember my paternal grandpa, Charles James Flower, well, although I was only a girl when he died. There is one exciting episode in his life, however, about which I can find out frustratingly little – despite expecting there to be a considerable amount of information about it in the public domain.

My grandpa was born in Camberwell, London, in 1882 and died in the north in 1966. He spent all his working life in the south of England. His father was an insurance agent and my grandpa worked in the same business in his youth. He moved into the newspaper industry just before the First World War, working in advertising at the *Daily News*, which later became the *News Chronicle*. Here he served as advertising manager until retirement in 1948. However, it was his wartime activity which really fascinated me. We have evidence to prove that these years are of interest as they led to his being granted the status of Honorary Freeman of London on 5 October 1945. We have in the family a scroll dated 11 February 1946 which, I suspect, is when the actual ceremony took place.

The Honorary Freedom of London is an honour indeed and one to be cherished. Over the years, many famous people from

Britain and overseas have been given it and it is something of which our family can be proud. Keen to find out more, I got in touch with the senior archivist at the London Metropolitan Archives at the Guildhall Library, London. He advised me to contact the clerk of the Chamberlain's Court who might have been able to provide more information about the award. I duly did as requested and the clerk was kind enough to respond and to describe my discovery as exciting, as it put grandpa on a par with greats such as 'Nelson, Wellington, Pitt, Churchill and Florence Nightingale'. He informed me that the award had been made because grandpa had been commander of the city's fire-guards in London during the Second World War. Mainly volunteers, the fire-guards' job had been to patrol the London streets checking for incendiary bombs and extinguishing them. The clerk also sent me general details of the award and the criteria for receiving it.

Obviously too old to have been involved in active service, grandpa appears to have a made a considerable contribution to the defence of London in and around the time of the Blitz. However, I have not, as yet, been able to find any newspaper references to the award ceremony, or any photos if any exist, or details of exactly what he did during the war. Sadly, the *News Chronicle* went out of circulation six years before his death, as this may have been a good place to look for an informative obituary. I'm hoping that there are still avenues left to explore in order to make a fairly recent ancestor even more interesting.

The Tale behind the Tale

Barbara Mason's story is a fascinating one. Family history can be frustrating at times – especially when it becomes difficult to find information on family activities that are relatively recent and would seem, at first glance, to be prime subjects for written evidence. There is still considerable hope that some more

Scroll for Charles Flower's Freedom of London. (Courtesy of Barbara Mason)

evidence will turn up in this particular case. The University of Sussex, for example, has an extensive archive (namely Mass Observation) of primary sources relating to the Home Front in the Second World War, and its online index is extremely helpful. Just as a taster, it has (in series 23/11/B Fire-fighting 1939–1941) selected leaflets and duplicate instructions, as well as written 'observations on fire-fighting activities in London'.

The publishers of the *London Gazette* were also keen to flag up success in the city during wartime and often featured medal citations for those given awards for work on the Home Front. Equally, the Guildhall Library may be worth revisiting as it has documents relating to firefighting in the city during the war which are catalogued separately from the archives dealing with the Freedom of the City. Barbara's grandpa may have an obituary somewhere, too – in a regional newspaper, a London newspaper or even a national one (after his retirement the *News Chronicle* was 'taken in' by the *Daily Mail*, for example).

38

THE RAG SORTER AT A WELSH PAPER MILL

by Keith Gregson

We do not know the exact name at birth of this ancestor, or even exactly when or where she was born, although there is a host of official documentary evidence for what was to prove a fairly lengthy life. Born in Ireland, at some point between 1802 and 1805, her Christian name appears variously as Eleanor, Norah, Ellen Norah and Annora. One source gives her exact birthplace as 'Innis, Waterford', but we have not been able to locate such a place. Her married name was Buckley and her husband Michael Buckley was born on the Cork coast. Details of their children suggest that they married in around 1830 in Ireland and moved to Wales around 1835. For the next half century she lived with her husband in the parish of Llangenny, close to Crickhowell and the Anglo/Welsh border. Her husband was an agricultural labourer throughout his working life in Wales and she was usually described as a labourer's wife – with one exception. At census time in 1851, when their address was the 'Factory, Llangenny', 'Eleanor's' occupation was noted as 'rag sorter in paper mill'.

Twenty or thirty years ago, finding further details on such an Irish/Welsh ancestor and her work would have been a mammoth task. The Internet has made life simpler here. The education authorities in modern Powys, for example, have put together a package on the history of Llangenny in Victorian times. When the Buckleys lived there, Llangenny's population hovered around the 500 mark – 'a rural border parish with a small population'. In 1841 there were seven poor people living in tents on the common with the remainder working on the farms or as servants in the 'big houses'. An online map for the period shows a fast-moving river named the Grwyne Fawr which, according to the same source, was used to power two paper mills.

Simply entering 'Welsh Paper Mills' into an Internet search engine gives immediate results, leading to a site packed with useful detail. According to another source, 'Eleanor' worked at 'Parry's Paper Mill', and a William Parry owned two mills in the parish at one point. Since one was at the hamlet of Glangrwyne in the parish, and the Buckleys' address was given in two censuses as 'Llangrainey', this would seem the most obvious. The mill here started operation in the middle of the nineteenth century in an old iron foundry and in 1850, the year before 'Eleanor' worked there, was producing 'brightly coloured shop or grocery papers'.

The type of work she may have been involved in is clari-fied by interviews carried out for the Children's Employment Commission of 1843, whereby inspectors visited a paper mill in Wrexham and found it peopled by boys, girls, men and women. The commission report notes: 'Women and girls did most of the rag sorting, cutting and dusting. Children worked at the glazing as well, while boys maintained the beating engines and called themselves engineers. The more skilled jobs were carried out by men.'

The Tale behind the Tale

Research into this ancestor's origins touched on many of the problems faced by all with Irish ancestry. 'Eleanor' appeared in five consecutive Welsh censuses and yet we are none the wiser about her birthplace. In 1841, as for all the Irish in England and Wales, it was simply noted as 'Ireland or foreign parts'. On three other occasions it was noted simply as 'Ireland', and in the one case that an exact location is mentioned, the place does not appear to exist. Even if an exact place were known, the likelihood of finding original documentation is very lim-ited. As is well known in Irish research circles, much material of genealogical interest was lost during 'The Troubles'. Today, various organisations are using the Internet to make available what is left and things are certainly improving on this front. Despite these efforts, Irish ancestral research still resembles looking for the legendary 'needle in a haystack'.

On a positive note, the Internet proved an invaluable aid when it came to researching this ancestor's life in Wales. One site has been especially set up to help schools in local history research. Such sites are on the increase and well worth looking out for – as are sites dedicated to the history of specific indus-tries in specific locations.

It is intriguing how ancestors such as the mysterious 'Eleanor' come to be paraded almost with pride, as in 'my ancestor sorted rags in a paper mill and I ended up gaining a university degree and teaching history'. This is a kind of reverse snobbery, which also turns up when the subject of historical family villains and anti-heroes is raised.

39

A CELEBRITY IN OTAGO

by Brian Butler

I started tracing my family tree quite by accident, not knowing who my grandparents were or anything about my family history at all. My parents did not speak about their ancestors and none of us ever made further enquiries. I was not interested in researching until my wife decided she was going to trace her tree. She was getting nowhere on hers so started on mine and she is now upset that mine has come on in leaps and bounds while hers is still leading her around in circles.

I discovered strong Kentish roots on both sides of the family but became particularly intrigued by a line of Pococks on my mother's side. One thing my mother did say in casual conversation was that she had a cousin in this branch who used to travel between Australia, New Zealand and England buying and selling. This led me to an ancestor by the name of Shadrach Edward Robert Jones – a real character who has left quite a mark on the history of New Zealand.

We know that Shadrach began life in Kent, as his grandfather, Robert Pocock, left an account of the youngster's christening:

Went to Gravesend Church and stood Godfather to my daughter Elizabeth's [Mrs Jones'] child, by naming it

Shadrach Edward Robert. The child's name was to please all parties: first Shadrach because my grandfather Pocock's name was such, the second name was to please the family of Jones, and the third name is my own.

The year was 1822.

Young Shadrach grew up to become a doctor, qualifying as an MD at St Andrews in Scotland in the 1840s. He married, and after working in Shropshire for a while, immigrated to Australia soon after the opening of the Gold Fields. While in his early 30s he set himself up in Bendigo as an auctioneer and stabler.

In 1861, after a short stay back in England, he headed for Otago in New Zealand, once again attracted by the 'gold fever'. Having settled in Dunedin, he opened a hotel and theatre, which became the talk of the town. He attracted top acts to the theatre including the world-famous Christy Minstrels. A real wheeler-dealer, he persuaded George Parr to bring his touring professional English cricket side across from Australia

Photograph of Shadrach Jones.
(Courtesy of Brian Butler)

WHO of those in Gisborne now who landed in Dunedin in its younger days does not remember Shadrach Jones of the Provincial Hotel. Eight bars ; eight pretty barmaids (six of them married to fortunes) ; takings, £800 a day ; expenses, L150 per diem for its management. Shakedowns everywhere —in the billiard rooms ; in the kitchen ; in the stables (the stables by night a theatre) ; in the landings ; in the passages ; —wherever a pair of blankets could be stretched there was an occupant at four shillings a night for the use of the flooring boards. Breakfast, four shillings ; dinner five, having to wait half an hour to get a plate of meat, even if it then could be got without one waiter snatching the plate from another. Shadrach went to England, stayed there twenty years, and is once more in Dunedin. Mr. Jones was, perhaps, the most widely known man in Otago in the days of the gold-digging excitement. He brought over the All-England Eleven to play cricket in Dunedin ; he took a leading part in organising the great champion race meeting, when the "big event" of 1000 sovs. attracted horses from Australia and all parts of New Zealand ; he had a great deal to do with the opening and carrying on of the celebrated Vauxhall Gardens ; and in numberless ways the name of Mr. Shadrach Jones was constantly before the public in connection with all kinds of movements, speculations, and organisations.

Obituary of Shadrach Jones. (Courtesy of Brian Butler)

for a short tour in 1864. This proved a financial disaster, mainly due to events beyond Shadrach's control, involving a fire and a storm. He lost heavily on the enterprise and had to leave the hotel business.

Unfortunately, he was unable to revive his fortunes when he took up auctioning. Obviously a restless soul, he upped sticks and travelled the world for the next sixteen years, only returning to New Zealand in 1882 when he began to practise as a doctor once more. He then moved to New South Wales in Australia where he died in July 1895.

Shadrach left enough of a mark on early New Zealand colonial history for his life story to be of interest to others. I picked up most of my information about him from a biography written by George Griffiths in a *Dictionary of New Zealand Biography*. Here Griffiths notes that Shadrach was a short, stout, ruddy-faced man, with side whiskers and curly, dark hair; and that he was remembered in Dunedin for his chequer-board waistcoat, fat cigar, lavish jewellery and bulldog at heel. He was clearly a man of many parts. He supported racing, sport and the hunt, wagered bets freely and lived for the moment. He was involved with the voluntary fire brigade and the Otago Light Horse (as a surgeon), and took an interest in the New Zealand Exhibition of 1865. In fact, somebody went so far as to describe him as 'New Zealand's first true entrepreneur' – quite an honour.

The Tale behind the Tale

Brian Butler's ancestor is well qualified to be in this book and is in many ways typical of the entrepreneurial spirit we associate with the Victorians and the heady days of Empire. He seems to have won some, lost some and to have shrugged his shoulders and moved on – more than once.

Brian's researches have been successful in terms of discovering useful printed and published materials. These include books containing details from a family diary (in connection with Shadrach's christening) and a fascinating physical description gathered seemingly from eyewitness accounts.

Equally intriguing is Shadrach's family life, which receives little mention in the published works. Brian's researches have led him to discover more about his wandering ancestor's wife and family. In the *Dictionary of New Zealand Biography* it is noted that Shadrach married a Louisa Onions in Shropshire in May 1845 and that they had eight children. Brian takes up the story:

I resolved to see what happened to Louisa. I could only find six children from the census records, not eight as previously mentioned. Louisa I believe stayed in the UK. She never remarried, as far as I can find out. On the census she always stated that she was the wife of an MD, although on one of the census returns (Lambeth, 1881) this was crossed out, and in her latter years she stated she was of independent means. She does not appear on the 1901 census.

Was Shadrach sending monies home? Did Louisa at some time emigrate or travel to and from Australia with her husband, even for a little while, and bring monies home? Were her sons bringing or sending monies home? Were they HIS sons and daughters on the census? Why is there an eleven-year gap between the last two children? These questions will have to be checked out further.

I know that Shadrach was staying with his eldest daughter, Alice, in Wrexham at the time of the 1871 census, his occupation stated as MD, Physician, Surgeon. At some time he was reported as 'whereabouts unknown' in Natal, South Africa, and if he did not register his address to the military authorities, his name would be removed from the Medical Register there. It was also reported that he owned a stud farm in South Australia. This story I am sure will continue to run as I find out more.

Absorbing questions and observations, and ones with which anyone with wandering ancestors will surely empathise. Certainly Brian's ancestor's contribution to New Zealand and indeed world cricket has not gone unnoticed. In his book *Cricket Around the World*, Anton Rippon notes that the visit of George Parr's side to New Zealand in 1864 was the first ever made by an English side. The games were played 'against the odds' (the home side had more players than the visitors). Such games attracted huge wagers, which fits in nicely with the picture of Shadrach painted by his descendant.

40

A LONG LINE OF COOKS
by Eileen Richardson (née Addison)

My husband was christened David Richardson and we are both from firmly settled Wearside families. When I began to research his family tree I thought I might have difficulty. Not only is the name Richardson one of the most common, but successive generations in the direct line named their sons either John or George. My father-in-law, however, remembered that when he was a child there was a Rogerson Richardson and a Nathan Richardson in the extended family and I thought that these names might be a good point with which to start my researches.

An early breakthrough came with information gained from the marriage certificate of David's direct ancestor, George Richardson, in Sunderland in 1854. On this certificate, George's father was given as Cook Richardson (deceased).

George Richardson went on in the 1860s to have six sons; among them were Cook, Rogerson and Nathan. According to the censuses of 1861 and 1871, George was a mariner or seaman in the merchant service, having been born locally around 1831. His wife was born in the port, too. The Rogerson and Nathan appearing here (born *c.* 1864 and *c.* 1866 respectively) will have been those remembered by my father-in-law from his youth.

Having Cook, Nathan and Rogerson Richardson as some unusual names to search for, I checked on the online Latter Day Saints IGI index and found that these names turned up in two places – Sunderland and Lincolnshire. There remained a problem. I couldn't find a George Richardson as the son of a Cook Richardson born in Sunderland around 1831 – and George had told the census enumerator that Sunderland was indeed his birthplace. However, the 1841 census records a family in Grimsby, Lincolnshire, consisting of Cook Richardson, 50; Mary Richardson, 47; and their children who include a Rogerson Richardson and another son George, aged 12. As ages in the 1841 census were approximate, this would fit in nicely with my husband's direct ancestor George.

The 1841 census records only one other Cook Richardson. This one was 75 and living in Frampton, Lincolnshire, with Mary Richardson, aged 65. It is probable that this Cook Richardson was the father of the Cook Richardson in the 1841 Grimsby census, as the IGI shows the baptism in October 1790 in Scamblesby, Lincolnshire, of 'Cooke' Richardson son of 'Cooke' and Mary Richardson.

I was now able to complete the cycle of names neatly, as it is likely that the elder Cook Richardson in the 1841 census is the one whose baptism is recorded in the IGI in 1765 at Baumber in Lincolnshire – father's name John Richardson. Again, taking into account the approximate ages given in the 1841 census, this would seem to fit perfectly.

They say that 'too many cooks spoil the broth'. This certainly wasn't the case with my husband's family! These particular 'Cooks' have helped me to break through a seemingly impenetrable barrier and to get my husband's family out of his native place and back into the rural east of England during the middle of the eighteenth century.

The Tale behind the Tale

In many ways this is one of the most absorbing pieces of research in the book and it provides us with a number of useful trails to follow.

In the first instance, we have another fine example of a wife following up her husband's family tree for her own interest and for the future interest of the family. Then, in terms of the sources used for research, there are multiple references to the Latter Day Saints IGI, free to use and accessible on the Internet and in most Local Studies Libraries. There are errors of both transcription and interpretation in some entries on this site, but it can still be massively helpful. Eileen Richardson used it to find the grouping of a specific set of names and was successful in discovering David's links back to Lincolnshire.

The Grimsby link makes complete sense in historical terms. Grimsby is a port lying on the much-used 'sea road' between London and north-east England. George and his wife could easily have met up when he was 'offloading'. Eileen's side of the family also has roots with the Norfolk port of King's Lynn, one of the next 'hopping off' points south of Grimsby. Researchers looking at families along the entire east coast of Britain ought to bear this in mind. From Shetland down to Great Yarmouth (and indeed beyond) there was a big mobile family of people linked to the working with the sea – and to fishing in particular.

One intriguing question remains, and one which should provide food for thought for all family historians. Why did George Richardson state on more than one occasion that he was born in Sunderland when Lincolnshire is by far the most likely reality? There are a number of possible answers. Firstly, as a merchant sailor, George was likely to be aware that local links had to be firm for his family to receive charitable relief and/or a place in Trafalgar Square. He will also have accepted the strong possibility of losing his life at sea. He served in the merchant service during the era of the 'sea coffins' when some shipowners were happy to overload old vessels and sink them for the insurance – sometimes with loss of life. The introduction of the 'Plimsoll Line' in the 1870s gradually put paid to this activity, but loss of life at sea was a real problem in the mid-Victorian period. In ports, widows and orphans overwhelmed the Poor Law system and some authorities looked to using the Laws of Settlement to cut down on expenditure. This would exclude help for those not born in the locality. Even though George's wife and children were Sunderland born and bred, if he were not, the Poor Law authorities might have had a case to make for not paying out after his death – particularly to his children.

Secondly, there is always a chance that George did not know where he was born, but this seems unlikely, and it is most probable that his white lie can be put down to sensible skulduggery. Ultimately, he was likely to have got away with his 'untruth' as he was born six or seven years before the introduction of birth certificates and so was not going to be asked to produce one.

41

REMOVED UNDER THE LAWS OF SETTLEMENT

by Keith Gregson

Direct ancestor Elizabeth Penrose (1763–1844) falls into a long line of my ancestors associated with Cornwall. For much of her later life she, her husband Thomas Penrose and their children lived in the Devon mining community of Mary Tavy.

In 1839 her husband died, and the Mary Tavy parish records reveal the remarkable tale of what followed.

When researching family trees prior to the age of the census and civil registration, the tendency is to head directly for parish records relating to baptism, marriage and burial. Other significant parish records may also have survived, and in the case of Mary Tavy, these were the records of the overseers of the poor.

The Penrose name had already turned up in the poor records before Thomas' death in 1839. In 1831, for example, there was a note to the effect that a Tregavethan parish owed Mary Tavy £9 16s for 'E Penrose and family', and there were 'extraordinaries' for her too in 1832 and 1833, which cost Tregavethan 16s on each occasion. After Thomas' death, further mentions began to hot up. There are references to 'law expenses on E Penrose £4-9-6', her 'removal to Kenwyn appealed against and superseded' and also to 'a letter from Truro respecting E Penrose' – though there is no sign of the letter itself. At Christmas 1839, the Mary Tavy overseers appealed for 'expenses for attending Tavistock on account of E Penrose to procure order superseded and appearance before magistrates for that purpose – 2/6' (2s and sixpence). Early in 1840, the same overseers received '£3-9-0 by cash from the relieving officer of Truro for E Penrose under a suspending order of removal to Truro'. The final reference appears on 24 June 1840: 'Expense for the overseer and Eliz Penrose for victuals and travelling expenses from Sunday evening until Thursday following – a pauper of this parish to the parish of Tregavethan in the County of Cornwall being removed under a suspending order – £4-3-0.'

Clearly something was going on, but more sleuthing was necessary in order to establish exactly what this was. The first thing to ascertain was the significance of all the places mentioned. In 1839 the Penroses lived in Mary Tavy, a parish in the Tavistock Poor Law Union, meaning that it was in Tavistock that all key decisions concerning the Poor Law of this district were made. Tregavethan was a small township next to or part of the parish of Kenwyn in Cornwall, which was itself part of the Truro Poor Law Union. The Truro Union also had its workhouse in Kenwyn.

Elizabeth Penrose had thus been 'removed' from Mary Tavy to the workhouse in Truro. The reason, although never noted down, must have been that she had no settlement in Mary Tavy and that her considered place of settlement was Tregavethan. Under the law of the day, that parish was still responsible for her if she became poor and asked for help.

Knowledge of such Poor Law practice can be of considerable value to the family historian, and can lead to evidence which might otherwise remain undiscovered. For instance, since Elizabeth was moved in 1840, could she still be in the Truro workhouse, Kenwyn, at census time in 1841? The answer is yes: aged 80 and 'born in the county'. Elizabeth lived for three more years and her death was registered at Truro in 1844 with the workhouse as her address and her age again given as 80 (the 1841 census gave ages to within five years only). In addition, had she married locally? Again the answer is yes: on 20 January 1794 Thomas Penrose married Elizabeth Harris at St Agnes by Truro, a neighbouring parish. Son Richard was baptised there in late March of the same year (a not uncommonly short gestation period). This son Richard was with them in Mary Tavy when the next child was baptised there in 1798; and records reveal that many of the Mary Tavy miners moved up from the St Agnes area in the 1790s. It all fits.

Could Elizabeth Penrose (*née* Harris) be traced further back in Cornwall history? A positive answer again: she was baptised in Kenwyn (which included Tregavethan township) on 23 July 1763, and had family there back another couple of generations. The Penroses were also traceable to Newlyn East, Cornwall, as metal miners in the early 1600s.

Tregavethan, the place which my ancestor proved so costly to, is still there; it is a case of 'blink and you'll miss it', consist-

ing of no more than a handful of buildings in a small wooded
valley.

The Tale behind the Tale

Elizabeth's tale is an excellent example of the close links
between research needed for family history and that required
for the study of a more general social and economic history.
It proved particularly exciting to research as it allowed me
to bring to bear my own postgraduate work in the field of
English Poor Law history.

This story is tied closely into the ancient Laws of Settlement
and the changes in the Poor Law which came about in the
1830s. Paupers were poor people who sought out and received
official help, and Elizabeth I had decreed years before that such
help should be given at parish level. Because there was a lot of
movement in the seventeenth century, the Laws of Settlement
were then introduced. These stated that if the poor became
paupers, their new parish could send them back to their place
of settlement to be looked after. Like many laws of the day
these were seriously flawed, particularly as they never defined
what was meant by 'place of settlement'. Most overseers took
it as the place where the person was born. Some parishes followed the laws but most didn't; it was up to the overseers. In
some places, settlement certificates were given out so you
could prove where you came from. These have survived in
some areas of England (Essex, for example) and can be an aid
to the study of family history.

All this information makes Elizabeth's case clearer. Even
when her husband was alive she needed help. Mary Tavy
decided to let her stay, despite her lack of settlement in the
parish, and claimed the money back from Tregavethan/
Kenwyn as was common practice. Then in the 1830s there was
a huge change in the Poor Laws, mainly in order to save the
ratepayer money. Parishes were gathered together into Poor

Law Unions with workhouses at the centre. Workhouses were to be used as a 'test' of poverty and, apparently unknown to many, the Laws of Settlement continued to operate beneath the surface. By 1840, the Mary Tavy overseer had to answer to the Board of Guardians at Tavistock. Thomas Penrose had died and his wife asked for help; Mary Tavy wanted to continue as before but Tavistock said no and she was sent back 'home' to the workhouse at Truro, where she would have gone had she still lived in Tregavethan.

There remain interesting points to ponder. Firstly, all the fuss and the transfer itself must have cost Tavistock guardians a lot of money, so why did they bother? It was probably done as a message to all the Cornish born in the Union that if they appealed for parish/Union help they would be sent back to their native parishes. Since few would want this, there would be fewer requests for Poor Law help and this would mean a greater saving to the ratepayer in terms of relief paid out.

Secondly, we should reflect on what a real bonus this type of material is for the family historian. As the only census Elizabeth appeared on was that of 1841, we would have lost her roots had she remained in Mary Tavy. The enumerator would have simply noted of her Devon/Mary Tavy status, 'not born in the county'. With her husband already deceased, this would have been the end of identifiable research into that particular family line. As it is, family misfortune opened up a complete field of evidence and enabled a link to be made back to the reign of Queen Elizabeth I, who introduced the Poor Laws in the first place.

42

THE JUMBLE SALE
JOURNAL DISCOVERIES

by Heather Taylor

My husband's ancestral relative, Joseph Liddell, was a man of many parts. He was born in rural County Durham in 1841, but by 1871 he was living near the centre of Newcastle upon Tyne with his wife, two children and a servant. There he ran an agricultural merchant's business and insurance agency from an office directly opposite Newcastle Central Station. A number of his daily business journals which include marginal notes about events outside work have survived, and these have left us with a beautifully rounded picture of a Victorian ancestor and his family.

In the trade directories of the day, Liddell and Hobson (his partner George Hobson) were described as corn, seed, oil cake, guano and implement merchants and agents for the Northern Fire and Life Assurance Company. Much of the work mentioned in Joseph's business journal involved organising transport by train, picking up and arranging for the payment of materials and setting up visits to discuss fire insurance – which was his main area of interest in the insurance world.

The notes in the margin tell us much about his life: he went on Conservative outings; hired lodgings for family holidays at Tynemouth; and visited the theatre to watch named plays and pantomimes. In May 1869 he took the family to see the original Siamese twins. On 12 July 1869 he noted 'with Ralph Moore at Newcastle – broke into own house'. He must have mislaid his keys. On 25 July 1873 he hired Roland Harrison and his company to perform at the Harperley Gala (Harrison

Household census record for the Liddells

Name	Relation	Marital Status	Gender	Age	Birthplace	Occupation	Disability
Joseph LIDDELL	Head	M	Male	40	Kyo, Durham, England	Agricultural Supply (Provision Dlr)	
Margt. LIDDELL	Wife	M	Female	31	Stanley, Durham, England		
John M. LIDDELL	Son		Male	13	Harperley Mill, Durham, England	Scholar	
Annie R. LIDDELL	Daur		Female	8	Newcastle, Northumberland, England	Scholar	
Ethel M. LIDDELL	Daur		Female	4	Newcastle, Northumberland, England	Scholar	
George H. LIDDELL	Son		Male	2	Newcastle, Northumberland, England		
Isabel LIDDELL	Daur		Female	1	Newcastle, Northumberland, England		
Mary Ann CAMPBELL	Serv	U	Female	25	Newcastle, Northumberland, England	General Serv	

Source information for table on previous page can be found as follows:

Dwelling	52 Park Road
Census Place	Elswick, Northumberland, England
Family History Library Film	1342218
Public Records Office Ref.	RGII
Piece/Folio	5051/96
Page Number	I

was a well-known Tyneside entertainer whose songs appear in nineteenth-century collections of north-east ditties). In December 1873 Joseph missed the train and had to walk to another station to get his ride home.

There are also entries which bring tears to the eye, such as the black etched entry of August 1869 noting the birth of a son and his death fourteen hours later.

Simple work diaries, perhaps, but they have given us all a real insight into family life in Victorian times.

The Tale behind the Tale

The 'Liddell Journals' turned up on a 10p book table at a jumble sale in Rothbury, Northumberland, in the 1970s. There were three of them dated 1869, 1873 and 1889, plus a handwritten insurance agent's ledger and two 'text' books used in the insurance trade. There were also loose papers including some of the firm's advertising material.

In the 1980s an article on the journals appeared in a local newspaper and a short series based on it was featured on local radio. Members of the Liddell family heard this and got in touch as a result. A number of them were already involved in family history research and had established a chain of interest across the world. Official documents already picked up by the family

DUNDEE—14, St. Andrew's Place.	LIVERPOOL—Tithebarn Street.
EDINBURGH—20, St. Andrew Square.	MANCHESTER—78, King Street.
GLASGOW—19, St. Vincent Place.	MELBOURNE—105, Collins Street West.

LONDON BOARD OF DIRECTORS.

WILLIAM MILLER, EsQ., M.P., *Chairman.*

GEORGE G. ANDERSON, Esq.	R. D. SASSOON, Esq.
DUNCAN JAMES KAY, Esq.	JOHN STEWART, Esq. (Director of the Im-
SIR CHARLES R. McGRIGOR, Bart	perial Ottoman Bank.)
HARVEY RANKING, Esq. (John Ranking and Co.)	WILLIAM WALKINSHAW, Esq.
WILLIAM MUNRO ROSS, Esq. (Cottam, Mortan, and Co.)	GEORGE WITT, Esq., F.R.S.

Bankers { THE NATIONAL PROVINCIAL BANK OF ENGLAND.
{ THE UNION BANK OF LONDON.

Solicitors—Messrs. LYNE & HOLMAN.
Medical Officer—Dr. EDWARDS, 20, Finsbury Square.
Surveyor—A. B. FREND, 44, Bedford Row.

FIRE DEPARTMENT—E. H. MANNERING, *Manager.*

LIFE DEPARTMENT { A. P. FLETCHER, *Actuary.*
{ JAS. VALENTINE, *Assistant Actuary.*

General Manager—A. P. FLETCHER.

Agents at Newcastle:

MESSRS. HOBSON & LIDDELL, 9, MARY STREET.

Advertising literature for Joseph's firm. (Author's collection)

named children mentioned in the journal, thus positively confirming the link between the family and the journal writer.

Of the many interesting topics appearing in the journals, two stand out. One is the number of references to servants – including an entire back page section in one journal. Joseph Liddell always kept servants but they came and went with alarming regularity (was he a tough employer or were they simply poor employees?) The other is the references to his firm's marketing of guano. Guano must intrigue anyone with merchant sea-faring ancestors, as it used to be transported from South America to the UK regularly in the nineteenth century. It is the finest sort of effective manure, produced in copious amounts by South American birds.

Heather Taylor notes that George Hobson, Joseph Liddell's partner, was also his father-in-law. She has a copy of George's will, and remarks: 'He was a wealthy man who left a Gross Estate £34,016 2/9.' The 2/9 (2s and ninepence) alone would have been a reasonable sum just over 100 years ago! Heather's personal fascination with Joseph Liddell and his work came about through a friendship with her husband's elderly aunt, who was Joseph's granddaughter and also a great raconteur.

43

CENSUS FAME

by John Clarke

My great-grandfather James Clarke (1833–1911) started and ended his days in Norfolk and lived a life filled with some sadness and a little drama.

He was the son of a blacksmith from Castle Acre in Norfolk and was living there with his mother and father in 1841. By the following census, he had become apprentice to his father's trade and was still living with his parents at the age of 17.

Ten years on and he had settled in Clapham, Surrey, where he was serving as a constable in the metropolitan police. He had married a Clapham girl, Caroline, and they had an infant daughter, Mary Ann Elizabeth. The family was still in Clapham ten years later again; James remained a police constable and the couple had added a son, George, to the family.

By 1881, James was back in Castle Acre with his family and working once more as a blacksmith. His 17-year-old son was an apprentice saddler and his 19-year-old daughter was living with them. By the next decennial census, James, now in his 50s, was 'living on his own means' in Weybourne in Norfolk, and the number in the house had reduced to three. Mary Ann Elizabeth was still with them – almost 30 and unmarried.

By the time of the 1901 census, the Clarke family of three had moved to Swanton Novers in Norfolk, where Caroline had become a shopkeeper 'at home' and on her 'own account', while James was a 'police pensioner'. The house was described as a 'shop' and the family had acquired a couple of male boarders: one in his 50s and 'living on means'; the other a coach painter aged 20.

Finally, in 1911 and aged 77 and 76 respectively, James was recorded as a 'pensioner metropolitan police' and Caroline as 'an old age pensioner'. Their daughter remained unmarried and was approaching 50, and they had a visitor in the shape of 23-year-old granddaughter Amy.

On the surface this seems a fairly ordinary life, but further research shows this was not quite the case. From James' police record we know that he joined up in 1855 and left in April 1876. The reason for his departure was 'bodily infirmity' and the story goes that this was the result of injuries sustained while chasing two thieves on Clapham Common. In 1876 his police pension was set at a healthy £39 per annum.

Family tragedy is also apparent from other sources. The 1911 census, with its 'new' layout, reveals that James and Caroline were married for fifty-five years and had six live children – of whom only the two who appeared in the censuses survived. The other four were all males; three died within a month of birth, while one survived for a year – with the causes of death ranging from jaundice through bronchitis, to premature birth and genetic disease.

The surviving daughter's tale is a sad one, too. Mary Ann Elizabeth suffered from nephritis all her life, which is why she remained with her parents and unmarried. Upon the death of her father in 1911 she moved with her mother to live with her brother George, who was married and resident in Great Yarmouth. The new arrangements were not suitable for Mary Ann Elizabeth and she was placed in the workhouse. When this was taken over by the army in the First World War, she was transferred to an asylum at Brentwood in Essex where she died in 1918, a year after her mother. Brother George died in 1943.

The Tale behind the Tale

John Clarke is a keen family historian, meticulous in his research and the presentation of all he has discovered about his family. What is most interesting about his great-grandfather James is in one sense his normality, yet, as John argues, there is a little more to it than that. The main reason we know so much about James and his family is because he was born in time to appear on the first thorough census of 1841, and managed to survive until the most recently published census of 1911, even if only just. Details thus gained allow us to take a close look at the pros and cons of the census – one of the most prized of genealogical sources.

One problem, which often emerges in relation to the census, is that of enumerator and census subject literacy. The writing of the enumerators is welcomingly clear on all but one of James' eight entries, and in this one case the writing is merely small and thus more difficult to interpret. However, the 1871 enumerator seems to have had trouble with the name of James' wife. It appears as Carrolin – which may have caused problems if this had been the only written information on her to survive. More interestingly, the family appears under the spelling of Clarke with an 'e' on five of the entries, and Clark without an 'e' on the remaining three. This should encourage us all to experiment with as many different spellings as possible before giving up on particularly elusive ancestors.

The extra information collected by organisers of the 1911 census also proves helpful towards understanding what happened to the Clarke children. The fact that the four unfortunate youngsters who died survived long enough to have both births and deaths registered is a plus for the family historian. Their short lives eked out in the 1850s and 1860s were dismayingly typical, and it is not unusual to find numerous youngsters dying – often due to genetic and sexually transmitted illness or, more alarmingly, in family blocks at a later age caused by an epidemic. This remained the case until advances were made in both curative and preventative medicine during the twentieth century.

Police records, available at The National Archives, also proved useful to John. The documentation here explains why a humble blacksmith was able to live off 'his own means' while only in his 50s.

John Clarke has photographs of the family homes in Weybourne and Swanton Novers (the latter as the 'village shop' and as the domestic home it is today). In addition, he has produced a fascinating twenty-four-page booklet titled *What's In A Name – Clericus to Clark* (ISBN 0-9542263-6-4), which should prove a good read for anyone with that most common of surnames somewhere in the family.

44

SLEEPING THROUGH A TRENCH RAID

by Keith Gregson

To have one First World War diary in a family is something to treasure – to have three, all written by brothers, must be considered a rarity. There are three such diaries in our family: my grandfather, Fred Stephens, wrote one, while older brother John and younger brother Charles wrote the other two. The three brothers were born in the 1880s in the Cumbrian metal-mining town of Millom. Their father came from Mary Tavy in Devon and moved up there (via Wales) in the 1870s with family members and many others from the same village. The boys' mother was of Cornish stock. Her father came from St Blazey, drove the mine engine at Millom and was a local preacher.

The boys' father did not want them to work in the iron mines and saw that they had a good education. When war broke out in 1914 they were all in their 20s: John (the eldest) was working at the Co-op in Liverpool; Fred in the Post Office in Barrow; and Charlie (the youngest) in a shop in Haverigg. One by one they went to war, endured conditions worse than those experienced in a metal mine and, whether it was legal or not, kept diaries.

My grandfather's experience of war was perhaps the broadest. Although the middle of the three brothers in terms of age, he was the first to join up. This he did in 1915 when he started training as a signaller in the Royal Engineers. In the summer he was sent in as part of the final push against the Turks in the ill-fated Gallipoli campaign. He arrived at the peninsula in early August and was on loan to the ANZACs at Anzac Cove during the attacks portrayed in the Mel Gibson film *Gallipoli*. Pinned down close to the beach, he soon fell victim to the weather and poor food and water supplies. On one occasion, he wrote: 'At this time and place we were all stricken down with dysentery and diarrhoea – had big doses of castor oil – ten times in one day and four at night – almost a human skeleton.'

After one of the ANZAC assaults on the Turks, my grandfather Fred had the thankless task of re-establishing communications across the battlefield: 'My officer and two of us went a mile and a half up through the gullies and they were strewed with killed and wounded.' In the end, the hot weather and consequent disease caught up with him, and in November 1915 he was returned to England on a hospital ship.

Three months later, Fred was back in the heat of battle – this time in the trenches on the Western Front. From March to June 1916 he was trained to carry out the dangerous task of crawling close to German lines to set up a microphone and amplifier. An accompanying officer/interpreter could

The Stephens boys – John (standing behind), Fred (left) and Charles (right) – safe home from the war, 1919. (Author's collection)

then work out what the enemy was up to. Once, Fred and his officer had a lucky escape when the Germans attacked over the top of their carefully hidden dugout: 'When we opened the barricaded door in the early hours of the morning we saw a Tommy on sentry duty and he was greatly surprised to see us there – said we'd been very lucky fellows.' He also used his wireless skills when Messines Ridge was being undermined and crawled under the hill in order to listen to the enemy above. He was actually in the vicinity of the ridge in June 1917: 'Only a mile from the ridge when it went up.' It is said that this explosion rattled windows over the Channel in Kent.

In the middle of one bloody battle near Ypres he made three separate attempts to restore battlefield communications by crawling into no-man's-land. 'It was a proper death trap,' he commented, 'and I was lucky to come out alive.' In November 1917 he was present at the first massed tank battle in history which took place at Cambrai: 'From our position [a tree] we could see the tanks in operation driving the Germans out of the wood and Canal Bank. It was a wonderful sight – about eight or a dozen tanks in a line.' Soon after this, he was struck down with appendicitis and was sent back to England. He subsequently spent time at the signalling school in Bedford and was demobbed from the army at Catterick early in 1919.

The Tale behind the Tale

Fred's brother John was captured in the Somme area during the German spring offensive of 1918, and his diary deals with his captivity in detail. One of his grandsons has the original diary and there are also other pieces of memorabilia relating to his captivity in the family.

Brother Charles' diary is the longest and most detailed. He spent most of the war in India, and although safe from enemy attack, he and his companions were open to disease and illness and many died in the great influenza epidemic at the end of the war. His original diaries are now with his grandchild.

These diaries proved extremely useful when I was a secondary school teacher, especially as there were accompanying photographs and documents which could be used in evidence-based exercises. One exercise was particularly rewarding as it highlighted a major problem we face both as family historians and social historians. While on board a ship bound for Gallipoli, Fred wrote a cheerful letter to his mother which said, 'Could do with about three months of this – a trip to Canada or Australia would suit me down to the ground', and, 'You talk about the Barrow to Fleetwood trips; they have nothing on this' (these trips were apparently the annual 'boys' outings' from Millom). In contrast, his diary was not so cheerful. Here he wrote of exposed and unescorted ships, crowded accommodation, sickness and submarine scares.

In the classroom exercise the diary and the letter were introduced as two separate accounts of the same experience written by different people, and pupils were only informed later that the same person wrote both the diary and the letter. After a short baffled silence, somebody usually drew the conclusion that Fred wrote what he really thought in his diary and told his mum a white lie in the letter so she wouldn't worry. Whatever the truth, it is a salutary reminder that we have to take care as to what we accept as factual or truthful when dealing with evidence left by our ancestors.

45

A CORAM BOY
by Sheila Halliday

One of my great-great-great-grandfathers was called Thomas Ethell (or Ithill). He lived from 1759 to 1842, married twice, fathered three children, had eighteen known grandchildren and at least forty male Ethell great-grandsons. He died at the age of 83 and though he never rose above the rank of servant, gained a certain prominence as his origins became surrounded by intrigue.

As a baby, Thomas was placed in the Thomas Coram Foundling Hospital in London, thus becoming what is known as a 'Coram Boy'. The records reveal that he was born on 3 August 1759 in the tiny parish of Prees, Shropshire, and that he was the base-born son of one Ann Smith. No record for a baptism of Thomas Ethell could be found in the parish but there is one for William, the illegitimate son of Ann Smith, entered in the Bishop's Transcripts for Prees. A bastardy bond in Shrewsbury Record Office also states: 'Ann Smith of the Parish of Prees, singlewoman, hath in her voluntary examination declared herself now to be pregnant and with child and that the said Francis Reynolds (of Hodnet) is the true and sole father thereof ...'

Francis Reynolds was a married man from a neighbouring parish and had no other children. Ann was fortunate in that the child's father acknowledged fathering the child – thus making the child more acceptable to the parish as it was unlikely to become a burden on parish funds.

On 3 September 1759, Ann Smith's son was admitted to Coram's Foundling Hospital. His registration reads as follows:

A male child about one month old requiring a wet nurse ... was admitted being given the number 13853 ... the child was born in Prees Parish (Shropshire) August the 3rd 1759 ... no 13853 named Thomas Ithill was sent to a nurse on 8 September 1759 with Mary Ward of St Mary Cray, under the Seven Oaks inspection of Dr Lane.

There is no record of how he reached London, but within a month of birth he was admitted to this hospital without the lottery of black, red and white balls (these were usually drawn out of a bag in front of the mother in order to decide upon acceptance or rejection of the child). Thomas' worldly goods consisted of a scrap of purple, patterned brocade material attached to a piece of paper, stating: 'This is to sattisfi the under Taker of this plase that all sides are Willing and The Child Was Born in Prees Parish august ye 3 1759 William Smith.' The note was signed: 'franses ranalls' and ann Smith (sic). Ann's signature is in a good round hand.

Thomas Ethell was then transferred to Westerham Hospital in Surrey on 21 April 1765. He returned to London on 24 August 1766 and was inoculated against smallpox in the same month, before being sent to Ackworth School near Pontefract in Yorkshire on 2 May 1768. Just over a month later, he was apprenticed to a farmer near Malton to be trained in husbandry; indentures were sealed. He later worked at Scampston Hall, probably as a day labourer. He was also described as a servant. Thomas died at Scampston at the age of 83 and was buried in the churchyard.

The story of the Coram Foundling Hospital alone is enough to make Thomas an interesting ancestor, but there is more. Indeed, there has always been a rumour which has never gone away that he was the illegitimate son of the future George III. There were already rumours in my family that we were in some way descended from royalty. Others, including the author Jean Plaidy, have hinted at the possibility of his being the son of the monarch and a Quaker called Anna Lightfoot. The link here was Ackworth School, which proved, at the time in question, to have been a northern annexe to Coram's institution. Also, by a strange quirk of fate, the wet nurse given to Thomas at Coram's had also suckled the children of George III.

In all honesty, I think it highly unlikely that I have royal blood in me as a result of my foundling ancestor, but I am more than happy to conclude my little piece with a thought-provoking 'we'll never know for certain'.

The Tale behind the Tale

Sheila Halliday's mother, whose life spanned the entire twentieth century, was an Ethell by birth, and her Ethell ancestor (Thomas' son) moved from Yorkshire to Kent to work in the shipyards at Chatham in the early nineteenth century.

Sheila's ancestor has been extremely well researched and her success points to the usefulness of fringe evidence such as bishops' transcripts of parish registers and bastardy bonds. The latter often turn up in archives in record offices.

There has also been a great deal of interest shown in the Coram Foundling Hospital in recent years in the form of books and television programmes. Sheila caught up with Pauline Litton, who had written about Thomas Ethell and the hospital in *Family Tree Magazine*, and was able to confirm her link to Thomas and also to Pauline. Pauline had also carried out considerable research into the origins of the school at Ackworth – an institution which still operates successfully as a boarding school today. Ackworth retains its Quaker roots and many of its pupils past and present display a keen interest in both religious and family history.

Among the most appealing aspects of the Coram institute is the display of memorabilia, such as the scraps which were left with a child as a form of identification, as are mentioned in this tale of Thomas Ethell.

46

PRESENT AT NAPOLEON'S DEATH

by Audrey Phizackerley (née Janes)

There is a painting hanging in Les Invalides in Paris depicting the last moments of Napoleon Bonaparte in exile on the Isle of St Helena. Kneeling on the right-hand side of the painting, head in hands, is allegedly my ancestor, Abram Noverraz.

I was born and raised in the Cotswolds of England but my mother was a Noverraz, a family with Swiss-French roots.

My grandfather, Louis Walter Noverraz, was born in rural Berkshire in 1855 and was taken back to Switzerland as a child, only to return with his mother to the Cotswolds as a teenager. The story goes that Louis' father had died as a young man in his 30s, and his widow had sold the family hotel in Lausanne in order to finance their permanent move back to England. The deceased father had originally come to England to work as a butler where he had met his English wife who was in service in the same house.

In many ways, the family hotel in Switzerland is key to the story. The family purportedly bought it with money Abram Noverazz received after Napoleon's death. Abram had served the former emperor as second valet and groom, which was a relatively minor position, yet Abram played a major role in the controversy surrounding Napoleon's death; research into which has flared up again in recent years. After his master's death, Abram shaved some hair from the body, and it is these samples that have been the basis for recent research into the mystery of the French emperor's death.

As a result of the fresh examination of the hair, there is now a school of thought that the emperor was poisoned – probably by strychnine. The main suspect is General Charles de Montholon, a confidant of Napoleon's on the island of St Helena. Due to a shortage of money he may have been persuaded to assassinate the former emperor – either by French royalists or by the British authorities hoping to remove any chance of yet another armed return.

A 2001 article from the *Daily Telegraph* sums up the state of research into Napoleon's death at the end of the twentieth century. Indeed, it certainly flouts the idea that he died of stomach cancer: 'For years de Montholon fed his leader wine laced with arsenic which made him ill but was not deadly. However, a mixture of an orange drink, bitter almonds and calomel created a lethal cocktail. Calomel added to arsenic produces strychnine which both kills then removes all symptoms.'

Napoleon Bonaparte. (Rev. J. Taylor, *The Family History of England*, Vol. V, London, 1890–1910)

The tales of our link with the death of Bonaparte and with the sale of the hotel were first told to me by my mother when I was young. She also indicated that Abram was a direct ancestor. Since then, a cousin of mine set about updating our family tree. He contacted the Swiss Embassy staff in London who told him that an Abram was born 'about 1767', which would make him in his mid-50s when Napoleon died in 1821. This male cousin of mine had just reached the point where he seemed to be getting somewhere, when he himself died.

The links to Switzerland make the research a little more complex, although I am sure somebody conversant with modern technology will come up with the answer sooner rather than later. What is certain is that there was a Noverraz at the emperor's side in St Helena. A book published in French in 1968 and transcribed into English thirty years later has a couple of references to a male Noverraz 'Swiss National employed in Napoleon's service' – also, intriguingly, to a Josephine Noverraz, a 'member of the paid staff of Napoleon'.

The Tale behind the Tale

Audrey Phizackerley's tale is another one passed down through a family which proved to have more than a little truth in it. The research has been made more complex by the Swiss connection, although the Internet has made life somewhat easier. Her cousin got little joy from the Swiss Embassy as the staff there were, naturally, unable to carry out anything in the way of detailed research. The family has also made a collection of the various newspaper articles, which appeared from time to time, discussing the nature of Bonaparte's death. It is interesting to note the word 'assassination' being used increasingly in such articles.

A quick Internet search of the current thought on Noverraz has moved the story on. One site suggests that Napoleon's man was one Jean Abram Novareez (sic), and that he lived from 1790 to 1849. He was third valet to Napoleon and was married in July 1819 to Josephine Broule who was in the service of the wife of the treacherous de Montholon. This makes it marginally more likely that Napoleon's valet was an ancestral sibling of Audrey's rather than a direct ancestor.

The subject of Napoleon's death is a continuing fascination. At one point in the ongoing discussions of the causes of his death, a suggestion mooted was that the arsenic came into his system via the wallpaper in his rooms on St Helena, although this interpretation now seems to be less popular. In the nineteenth century arsenic was certainly used in wallpaper manufacture, as it was in the flavouring of sweets.

47

THE ANCESTRAL RECIPE BOOK

by Betty Gregson (née Stephens)

Eliza Rosevear (1868–1933, unmarried) was my stepmother's aunt. She was part of a Cumbrian mining family that moved up from St Austell, Cornwall, in the latter part of the nineteenth century. Towards the end of Victoria's reign, she took up a number of jobs around Cumberland and Lancashire, including one as cook for a surgeon and another one running a bakery.

In my youth, Eliza's handwritten recipe book, which she had given to her niece (my stepmother), was in constant use

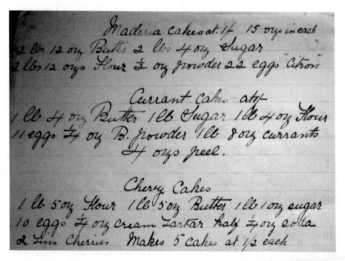

Excerpt from Eliza Rosevear's handwritten recipe book. (Author's collection)

around our house, particularly in the 1930s and during the Second World War. I think we must have inherited it after her death. My stepmother added one or two of her own recipes and I did too, so what we have now is a real family recipe book with entries stretching back well over 130 years.

There are some 300 recipes in the book as it stands; about 200 of them are in Eliza's hand and a number of them are specially geared towards Christmas. Three of these recipes were clearly aimed at mass production for the bakery and included a 'Best Xmas Pudding' at 1/- (5p) per lb, 'Xmas Cakes' at 8*d* (about 3p) per lb, and 'Christmas Cakes'. The Best Xmas Pudding had sixteen ingredients in total:

2lbs suet	1lb breadcrumbs
1lb flour	½ lb chopped almonds
1 ½ lbs raisins	1lb sultanas
2 ½ lbs currants	2 ½ lbs mixed peel
2 ½ lbs sugar	10oz spice
rind and juice of two lemons	
and four oranges	nine eggs
2 ¼ oz salt plus milk	rum and sherry or brandy

In 1937 my stepmother baked a special Coronation Cake. I think it was for Edward VIII in the first place but did just as well for George VI after the abdication of his brother. It really was a right royal recipe and had the following ingredients:

½ lb self raising flour	6oz fresh butter
6oz brown sugar	½ lb sultanas
½ lb currants	¼ lb glace cherries
¼ lb candied peel	3 fresh eggs
1 tablespoon milk	¼ tablespoon nutmeg
1 ½ oz almonds	
(ground or chopped)	1 tablespoon milk

What a contrast to another recipe from wartime which my stepmother took down from a neighbour and called 'Mrs Coulton's Good Christmas Cake 1944':

2 Cups plain flour	1 Cup sugar
1 Cup water	2 Cups mixed dried fruit
2oz margarine	2 t baking powder
1 t soda bicarb	

Boil fruit, water and sugar for a few minutes and allow to cool – add fruit and flour alternately and b powder last – do not mix too thin.

These are the instructions which accompany this recipe as mum did her best to bake something under the restrictions of wartime rationing.

Glancing back through the book today, I can see all sorts of interesting entries – especially in the back where Eliza wrote down 'recipes' for some remarkable concoctions. According to the flyleaf, all recipes in her handwriting were 'recopied' by her in 1902 when she was in her mid-30s, and it is safe to assume that they had already been in use for some time.

Her salad cream was made up of 'the hard boiled yoke of an egg rubbed up with a teaspoonful mustard, salt, sugar, cayenne, 2 tablespoonful salad oil and about 3 tablespoonful vinegar. Beat them all together and add a pennyworth of cream. Be sure to add the oil before the vinegar.' Furniture paste could be put together with 'one oz Castille Soap, 2 oz beeswax, half an oz of white wax shredded fine'. The ingredients were to be 'put in the oven to dissolve'. You then had to 'add a gill of boiling water, stir till really cold then add a gill of turpentine'.

Her advice on green peas still works today – simply 'add one teaspoonful of raw sugar' in order to 'keep the colour'.

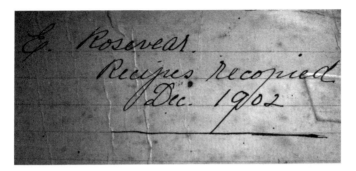

Flyleaf in Eliza's handwriting. (Author's collection)

The Tale behind the Tale

Betty Gregson's family recipe book is another gem and a fine example of material that is useful to both the social historian and the family historian.

Using this battered old book, the social historian has a lovely insight into what was produced in a late Victorian bakery and the type and amount of ingredients involved. The book also provides an overview of the way families coped with rationing during the Second World War. The little remedy recipes are of use to the social historian, too. Supermarket shopping has killed these off and it is fascinating to note that Eliza also made up her own horseradish sauce, cough mixture, bleaching liquor and embrocation cream!

For the family historian, books such as this add yet more flesh to ancestral bones. We have the professional cook and baker passing on her expertise to others in the family and signs, via the recipe book, that members of the family were also prepared to experiment with cooking and baking. This was not true in the case of all families, and social and economic history books show that, in the industrial cities at least, working mothers had little time to cook and experiment and found the development of tinned and convenience food a real blessing. This was the case from the nineteenth century onwards.

An examination of the book's contents with my mother also led to a new family tale. Mrs Penny, a next-door neighbour, had provided a 'recipe' for treating eczema and this reminded my mother of a wartime incident. Mother's family and the Pennys were both in their respective air-raid shelters on a particularly bad night. As the 'all clear' went, Mrs Penny popped her head out and cheered. In response, my grandfather popped his head out too and played the national anthem on his mouth organ. Another tale for the files as I didn't know my grandfather could play a musical instrument and would not have discovered this had it not been for Mrs Penny's recipe. As the television advert informed us, 'It's good to talk'.

HOW TO FIND YOUR OWN INTERESTING ANCESTORS

These case studies, and the tales behind them, provide useful facts and information which the family historian has used to analyse and draw conclusions from. These can further help when deciding how to approach a query about an unsolved mystery in your own family history, or where there appears to be little information available. Here is an outline of some of the ways in which you can directly apply the experiences of other researchers to help your own family history research.

Using Sources in Family History

Oral Sources

One of the soundest pieces of advice I was given when setting out to study family history was 'talk to as many older members of the family as possible'. From tales recounted in this book, it is clear that the oral sources thus gathered can be invaluable; write it down or record it for later reference. In his tale about the Lambourn arsonist (Chapter 2), Dennis Knight shows how his research interest was aroused by the story of an errant ancestor told to him by his mother when he was in his youth. Brian Pollard had both his father and older sister to thank for information on his grandfather's key role in a human pyramid, performing in an Edwardian music hall (Chapter 36). Carol Appleyard has fond memories of her grandfather (Chapter 3) which were verified by discussions with her aunt, whilst Audrey Phizackerley can clearly recall her mother's stories linking her Swiss ancestor to the death of Napoleon Bonaparte (Chapter 46). Similarly, our 'family friend' remembers with glee the family tale of how her naughty aunt and uncle made Queen Victoria laugh in the queen's old age (Chapter 21).

Then there are the raconteurs – the family storytellers. At times their tales can be tall and embellished, but other family members can be consulted for confirmation and supporting written sources sought out where any exists. Without such storytellers we would not have the tale of how great-uncle Billy came face to face with Admiral Togo of the Imperial Japanese Fleet (Chapter 7), or the true story behind the wedding photograph that never was (Chapter 4).

Particularly useful here are the community historians who can be found in smaller rural and island communities. Reference was made in a couple of case studies to the work of Alex Haley and his book and television feature series *Roots*. The publication and production covered the story of how a black American traced his ancestry through family tales of slavery to a village in Gambia. Here, a village historian recounted and reconfirmed the exact family tale of how the American's ancestor had come to be taken into captivity. A similar historian existed on the small Shetland island of Burra in the 1970s (Chapter 15). He was able to relate an island ancestry specifically and also to give details of a family nickname (the members of the family involved were known by all on the island as 'taingies' as they lived on a small spit of land called the 'Taing of Houss'). In a similar way, Margaret Weston had the good fortune to come across a knowledgeable sexton while searching for the grave where both her ancestor and his severed leg were buried (Chapter 14). This parish officer was able to add considerable colour to her story with tales culled from village gossip.

Elderly friends of grandparents or great-grandparents can also be a valuable resource. Carol Appleyard sought out a work mate and personal friend of her mining grandfather when writing her memoir and gained much useful information from him. Indeed, oral history is shown to have an important role to play in families where there is a strong core concept of family and heritage. This is the case with the Heron family of the Anglo/Scottish borders (Chapter 19 and Chapter 20), an area where family loyalty overrode everything else in times past. Not only is the story of the 'death on the moors' reasonably well known throughout the family (except apparently in New Zealand), but a much older tale has survived. It is of a married medieval Heron lady who turned down the approaches of a king on the night before a battle, with dire consequences – a tale with more than a smattering of evidential support and linked in fact to the medieval Battle of Otterburn.

Members of the Liddell family, originally based in rural England, have also kept in contact with each other despite immigration to Canada (Chapter 42). So, too, have those with links back to the wily 'Great Grenadier', who is known throughout the family as 'that old rogue', or simply as 'GG' (Chapter 30). Although migration may have divided families over the years, the Internet has helped to bring them back together. One feature of this has been the broadening out of those 'One Name Societies' which were already in existence. It was an interest in such a society that brought Tam Llewellyn-Edwards to the remarkable and elusive Jacques Samuel Fear and to his dark tale of 'adultery, incest and subterfuge' (Chapter 6).

Human longevity (or rather brevity) dictates that oral history should have a relatively brief shelf life when examined in the broader context of human history. Family historians now collecting their pensions will recall stiff old men proudly marching, bedecked with medals and able to provide tales of the bloody conflict that was the Boer War. Today, those marching thus saw service in, and are able to provide tales of, the Second World War. As generations progress we lose the ability to record these tales; indeed, we have reached the end of an oral resource with the deaths of the last of those actively involved in the foremost 'total war', the First World War.

Written Sources

One of the great developments in history education in England came in the 1970s, with the birth of the Schools Council History project. This promoted the study of research techniques in history lessons. All those educated in that period and thereafter have been made aware of the importance of studying primary history sources – sources 'produced at the time being studied'. These primary sources, and especially the written ones, are of immense value to the family historian and the tales in this book bear this out.

Within a short time of starting out, every family historian becomes aware of the mass of primary source material available since the Victorian period. From the middle to late 1830s onwards, there have been the records of civil registration (birth, death and marriage certificates). After 1841 we have the fairly full decennial censuses, and from the 1850s standardised will-making for those who needed one. Prior to this and continuing in many instances thereafter, there were the various church records of baptism, marriage and burial – resources which, in turn, elate and depress the historian depending on their condition and, indeed, very survival. Without these resources, the majority of the tales in this book would never have appeared in print – and there are other written resources of importance, too.

The Victorian period saw a massive increase in the number of newspapers – both local and national. As the nineteenth century wore on, publications also increased in frequency. Some of the contributors to this book were able to turn to such newspapers to find details of the trials and punishments of errant ancestors. This was the case for Dennis Knight and his Lambourn arsonist; Alison Lawson and her wandering murderer (Chapter 10); and Tam Llewellyn-Edwards whose ancestor was tried 'in absentia' for adultery and incest.

Similarly, when Anne Roberts found time to follow up the family story of a Victorian death in a snowstorm on the

Northumbrian moors (Chapter 19), she headed for the local paper and was instantly successful. Our 'family friend' is also able to confirm that her relatives 'amused' Queen Victoria, as this family tale found its way into a weekly newspaper on the Isle of Wight. Linda Hall discovered some accurate information about the activities of her less-than-honest 'Great Grenadier' by consulting a number of contemporary articles; and local newspapers in Barrow in Furness were consulted for evidence of a visit to the port and shipyards by Japan's 'Lord Nelson', Admiral Togo.

Great use can also be made of newspaper obituaries. Although something of a rarity for the majority of ordinary folk – certainly before the twentieth century – they might turn up if an ancestor has achieved anything of note or notoriety. The publication of the brief obituary of a farm-labourer ancestor in a late nineteenth-century Derby newspaper came as a total surprise (Chapter 34). All he had done was to live a lengthy life and to have resisted sleeping a single night of his life beyond the confines of his family home. Although fairly short, this obituary is packed with useful detail about the family and took further researches back to medieval times. Master mariner George Pottinger met with an untimely death at sea in the mid-Victorian period, as did many merchant seamen. Well known in his local community for deeds of bravery at sea and fast passages across the Atlantic, a number of different versions of the same obituary were published in regional newspapers (Chapter 9). As a child, Karen Foy was told frequently that a relative had been the voice of Mickey Mouse, so it was highly likely that his death, when it came, would be widely recorded. This proved the case and his obituary revealed an involvement in other equally famous Disney projects (Chapter 5).

In some cases, the written work of individual ancestors can turn up in newspapers. Kelsey Thornton's grandfather was of interest to his grandson due to his experiences as a cavalryman in the Boer War. Later, this grandfather became editor of a newspaper and this is where Kelsey discovered a descriptive account of his ancestor's war experiences (Chapter 18). Ancestors with pretensions as poets and feature writers also had material published in newspapers and magazines, and often wrote tales which throw further light on their family life. This was true in the case of 'Poet' Close (Chapter 23) and Robert Anderson, 'The Cumberland Bard' (Chapter 16).

Still in the realms of historic news coverage, reference is made in the main text to the important recent advances in Internet technology. Many magazines and newspapers from the nineteenth and twentieth centuries can now be consulted online, and names of ancestors discovered in articles at the press of a button. The story of Joseph Webbe Cragg (Chapter 28) was built up almost entirely through the process of searching 'Google Books'. When the research began, the family had no knowledge of an Indian connection at all, and the Internet came up with a wealth of evidence for such a link. The cause of his death only came to light recently, when a 'new' nineteenth-century publication was placed online. This confirms the need to constantly revisit the Internet with old questions.

In some cases, families have managed to hang on to ancestral journals and diaries and these have proven invaluable in helping to build up pictures of family life. The Swaddles, originally from County Durham and industrial Tyneside, are now spread around the world, but the two large journals written by one family member from 1867 onwards (Chapter 8) have roused considerable historical interest. They contain around 60,000 words and deal with many different aspects of social, working and family life in his native north-east England. Victorian businessman Joseph Liddell likewise kept a desk diary at work and his descendants are now pleased that he had a tendency to jot down little reminders relating to the family and his interest in sport. Certainly these sport entries really brought the diaries to life. One further case study deals with three brothers who kept diaries of their experiences during the First World War. All these diaries remain with the family. The major one featured here (Chapter 44), although not massively detailed, allows for a general overview of life on the beaches of Gallipoli and in the trenches of the Western Front. With the recent deaths of some of the last of the First World War campaigners, diaries such as these are increasing in historical value.

Ancestral letters can also be revealing and useful when building up a family history. Eileen Hopper's decision to package together letters sent to her husband's seafaring ancestor is one which has been very helpful when it comes to building up a picture of the experiences of Victorian master mariners (Chapter 11). The rediscovery of letters sent to his grandfather in hospital during the Boer War prompted Kelsey Thornton to actively research his ancestor's part in that campaign.

Earlier reference has been made to the importance of wills in genealogical research. Before the middle of the nineteenth century the established church was responsible for wills in England. Few people needed a will and regional organisation was massively complex. Where wills have been made and have survived, however, they can be very helpful. The case of an early eighteenth-century will made out by a tenant farming ancestor in Derbyshire proves this. Along with its accompanying inventory of possessions, the will provided the researcher with a rounded picture of life in one branch of the family (Chapter 24). By referencing later and more common wills, Lee Wotton (Chapter 25) discovered that his ancestor was a beneficiary in the will of the famous scientist and inventor Michael Faraday. Young Ben Shirvinton found out what happened to the family clock and also to the property and possessions of two of his farming ancestors (Chapter 26).

The case studies in the book also indicate that other 'official' documentation has its uses for the family historian. The Poor Law, both in its old parochial form prior to 1834 and in its new Union form post-1834, has left a mass of useful records, and both the donors and recipients of Poor Law relief frequently turn up in them. In the case of a family based in Devon and Cornwall, local Union and parish records provided information on a Poor Law settlement case. This allowed for the tracing back of one migrant family well beyond the days of civil registration (Chapter 41).

The Royal Commissions set up by various governments in Victorian times produced a wealth of useful written material on social and working conditions. Often published in the form of question and answer, the discourse collected can be found in bound volumes in study centres and, increasingly, online. Thousands of witnesses were called upon to give evidence and the vast majority of these witnesses will have had descendants. One such Shetland witness provided two vivid accounts of the living and working conditions for himself and other family members during the nineteenth century. Royal Commission findings can also be used to build up a picture of the type of life experienced by an ancestor, even if that particular ancestor was not a witness. When studying the life of a female Irish/Welsh ancestor described as 'a rag sorter in a paper mill', attention turned to a royal commissioner's visit to a similar nearby Welsh paper mill in order to discover more about the type of work involved (Chapter 38).

Official army records are very helpful and were used by Kelsey Thornton in his Boer War researches and also in my own research on ancestral diaries from the First World War. Official merchant navy log books have also survived in large quantities (although many British ones are now stored abroad) and these proved handy for researching two of the tales told in the book (Chapter 9 and Chapter 11).

Perhaps the most interesting of the primary written resources are the more unusual ones. A collection of old sheet music (Chapter 32) can tell us a great deal about the person or persons who put it together. A handwritten recipe book, built up over more than a hundred years, provides an insight into a family's eating habits (Chapter 47). Unpublished poems can also contain information on family members and friends, as the descendants of Victorian metal miner Thomas Gregg discovered (Chapter 31). In this context, the remarkable survival and discovery of an early eighteenth-century ancestral shopping note must surely rate as the icing on the cake (Chapter 1).

Efficient family history also necessitates the use of secondary written sources. Produced at a later date and reliant upon researched primary sources, these appear mainly as books, booklets and articles. Many of the characters mentioned in the studies had already attracted the attention of other researchers – and not only family historians. Consulting such works not only saves time, it also provides clues as to where to look for further primary source material. There are too many cases to mention in detail, but it is easy to find out more about Admiral Togo (Chapter 7), the Gretna Green Rail Disaster (Chapter 12) and Michael Faraday (Chapter 25) by turning to secondary sources such as reference books. The Internet also provides details on numerous secondary written resources and, in some cases, publishes the complete text of the resource.

Pictorial Sources

Primary pictorial sources have an important role to play in the construction of any family history, with photographs being particularly desirable and useful. Photography was experimental in the early nineteenth century and came into its own with the coverage, often gruesome, of the Crimean War in the 1850s and the American Civil War in the 1860s. Family photographs from the mid-Victorian period onwards are not all that uncommon.

The tales told in this book feature a number of photographs of military subjects covering a lengthy period in history. We thus have clear portraits of the 'Great Grenadier' from the Crimean War; a yeomanry officer in the Boer War; and four who served in the ranks in the army during the First World War (Chapter 9, Chapter 27). Posed photographs of young men in uniform during the First World War are relatively common, as it was practice to visit the local studio as soon as a uniform was acquired. It is only to be hoped that a name (and hopefully rank, regiment and number) was placed on the reverse of the picture when printed.

Wedding photographs were also fairly common. In some cases (and this applied to sporting photographs, too), they were hand-coloured from the late Victorian period. This was the case with the wedding photograph of 1894 (Chapter 4) – a photograph which held a number of surprises in store.

Others featured in these tales would have visited studios for formal photographs; for example, mine engine-winder Mark Swaddle and master mariner Joseph Scrafton. In many cases the name and address of the studio is printed on the photograph and this can be helpful when efforts are being made to pin down ancestral whereabouts. Captain Scrafton's photograph must have been taken when his vessel, the *Mary Ada*, put into the Italian port of Verona. There is also a very early photograph of Eleanor Heron who died in the snow on the Northumbrian moors and a much later photograph of Granda Gib with one of his much-loved pit ponies. In Edwardian times, it became fashionable to turn photographs of individuals and groups into postcards and these are also worth looking out for.

Those with maritime ancestry may be able to access useful pictures of seagoing vessels. These were frequently photographed or painted by marine artists (Chapter 7), making it a worthwhile exercise to put the name of a vessel into search engines such as 'Google Images'.

Before the days of photography, we have to rely on paintings, prints, sketches and miniatures, although in general terms only the rich and the successful are likely to have been thus depicted. Robert Anderson, 'The Cumberland Bard', died in

1833 before the establishment of photography, yet his works were important enough for him to be both painted and sketched.

Objects as Sources

One of the complaints made by those studying prehistoric times is that their research is restricted to objects alone. Without the benefit of contemporary writing, they have to work out for themselves the nature and purpose of the objects they find. Luckily for family historians, this is not usually the case, and there is often written back-up for the objects that turn up in the course of researches. Thus the military hat with the bullet hole recalled by Kelsey Thornton has written and oral sources surrounding it; sources which enabled Kelsey to recount the accompanying tale.

Many of the 'objects' valued by family historians might also be classified as written. This applies particularly to gravestones and memorial stones. Anne Roberts uses both in her tale (Chapter 19), and Margaret Weston's researches lean heavily on a gravestone in a Midland churchyard, which serves as a form of memorial (Chapter 14). In addition, a Quaker ancestor from the seventeenth century is remembered by a modern statue (Chapter 35).

Other objects of interest in these tales include a flute belonging to a poetic ancestor (Chapter 16) and the 'scraps' belonging to those placed in London's Coram Foundling Hospital many centuries ago (Chapter 45).

The Problems with Sources

The English Schools Council History project of the 1970s mentioned above had more than one string to its bow. Not only did it teach the value of primary source material, it also alerted pupils to the problems raised by using different types of sources as evidence – oral, written and pictorial. The tales told in this book reflect some of the pitfalls of using sources and, in some cases, prove beneficial in helping us to overcome resultant difficulties.

In the case of oral sources, we have to be aware that the memories of older folk (and some younger ones, too) are not always 'up to scratch' and can be selective. If we are trying to put together a picture of a fairly recent ancestor, for example, we ought to paint it 'warts and all'. This may not be easy or even possible, as at times some ancestral doors may remain firmly closed. Carol Appleyard's memories of her grandfather are all fond, as are those of the other friends and relatives she consulted. Could there perhaps have been another side to Granda Gib? In this case, the answer may well be 'no', but it is wise to speculate.

Then again, as the 1970s' history course pointed out, not all written sources provide reliable evidence. A number of tales in this book are based on journals and diaries, and it is a good idea to work out how and why these were written. Did the writer deliberately set out to paint a positive personal portrait for posterity and thus decide to leave out the nasty bits?

Then there is the question of telling the truth – not everybody does or did that. The Great Grenadier did not deny the deeds of bravery attributed to him when he patently hadn't carried them out, and he also had opportunities to tell everybody the truth. Certain family members also had a reputation for being economical with the truth when it came to age and place of birth. Chapter 6 demonstrates where the odd white lie can often be explained. One notably trustworthy ancestor, on the other hand, told a deliberate lie: according to his diary he was massively uncomfortable on his sea journey to a First World War battlefront; yet he still sent his mother a letter saying that he was having a great time (Chapter 44). If the letter alone had survived, we may have been led down the wrong path when coming to conclusions about his experiences. Fortunately, many of the tales told here are based on what might be called 'unconscious' jottings, where writers were simply noting down what was important to them with little comment – or thought that it would be read by others. Such material is handy as it allows us to make up our own minds about the character of the writers (Chapter 8 and Chapter 42).

Continuing the theme of 'bending the truth', it would seem that such activity also came from a healthy suspicion of bureaucracy. Government was growing at all levels from the eighteenth century onwards, and many ordinary people began to ask why detailed information was required for civil registration certificates and census returns. If the truth was likely to lead to economic loss, then it was safer to be 'economical' with that truth (Chapter 40). We also have to hope that ancestors were generally truthful when asked to declare family relationships. DNA testing is now proving popular in genealogical circles but it may well pose as many questions as it manages to answer (Chapter 13).

Findings by the Royal Commissions have to be handled with a little care. It is known that mill and mine children chosen for interview had to be persuaded out of their Sunday best. Rough work clothes were the order of the day as the reformers, who also coached many of the youngsters, hoped to paint the worst picture possible. Research has shown that mill and mine owners were not universally cruel, and it has been argued that the most astute and selfish owners worked out that a greater profit was to be gained with a contented workforce – although Karl Marx may not have agreed with this view. These problems noted, the Royal Commission evidence used in this book does appear fairly reliable. For instance, other reliable written evidence backs up Walter Williamson's Royal Commission account of life on nineteenth-century Shetland.

With continued reference to written evidence, considerable frustration can be caused by the inability to put a date to a significant event in an ancestor's life. This is especially true when an occasion might be thought to have provoked coverage by the local press. Today, many Local Studies Libraries and repositories have indexes to local newspapers, but the event you are seeking may take up only a few lines and be an unlikely candidate for indexing. The solution to this problem is not appealing; it might necessitate spending tedious hours trawling through newspapers. This is the case when researching a newspaper interview with a direct ancestor, which may have appeared in a Derby newspaper at some point in the 1880s (Chapter 34).

Some areas of the British Isles present their specific problems when it comes to ancestry. In Scotland, for example, civil registration came at a later date than in England and Wales, although the information on certificates is generally more informative than on similar certificates south of the border. Irish ancestry breeds its own frustration – and not all the causes are to be found on the western side of the Irish Sea. Again, civil registration started later and much vital earlier material has been lost through conflict, but the lack of thoroughness of English census enumerators plays a part here, too. The simple notification of a birthplace as 'Ireland' is not helpful and has brought research into many an Irish ancestor to a swift and unsatisfactory conclusion.

Another message from the tales is not to leave the questioning of relatives too long. Elderly relatives are not around forever and many family historians wish they had noted down what was said about the family in the past and regret not asking one or two more pertinent questions. Take the case of a close contact who now believes that a direct relative, deceased in the 1930s, wished to share a family secret with her shortly before death. A veiled hint was given and missed and, by the time the penny had dropped, the relative had passed on, taking the secret with her. Without going into too much detail, her tale may have solved what remains a baffling Victorian family mystery.

It may now be too late to take detailed notes from the First World War generation, but many who survived the second conflict are still around with time on their hands and a willingness to talk.

To carry the argument a step further, younger family historians should now be asking questions of the 'ageing generation', members of which should be noting down their past experiences with some of the following questions in mind:

What was it like for a baby boomer in the 1950s under the new National Health Service?

Did the Sixties really swing?

Where were you when Kennedy was assassinated, when man first landed on the moon and England won the Football World Cup?

Is this really history? I'm afraid it is and it needs to be noted down – now.

Pictorial evidence has its own pitfalls. 'The camera never lies' we are told, yet what the photographer puts in front of the camera may not be the truth. Equally, composites could be made up from originals to reflect what the photographer (or the purchasers of the photograph) wanted to happen. This was true even in the early days of photography. A classic example is two photographs taken of one of the early 'Barnardo Boys': one a 'before' with the boy scruffy and ragged; the other 'after' with the same child well-fed, clean and polished after years in a Barnardo's Home. In fact, the two photographs were taken in the same studio on the same day. What are we to make of this and what are we to make of family photographs taken on a special occasion? Is this really what our ancestors looked like? And remember that the Victorians in particular always kept a 'best side' for the photographer. As far as photographs are concerned, the 'fake' family wedding picture from the 1890s in Chapter 4 should provide warning enough.

Can we Really Discover what our Ancestors were Like?

The discovery of each new ancestor brings with it a combined wave of joy and frustration. There they are – a name in some ancient parish register or on one of the civil registration certificates, but often just a name, and with added luck a date or two and possibly an age, an address and an occupation. But who were they, what were they like and – in many cases a key question – am I like them?

In many instances these questions cannot be answered, yet some of the tales told in this book must give us encouragement and at least persuade us to keep on looking. Particularly interesting are those featuring ancestors who, for one reason or another, wrote things down. Some of their works were published, some were not, while others still simply jotted down their thoughts, deeds and daily doings for themselves. These writings provide us with close details on men who were metal miners, sailors, fishermen, weavers, carpenters/joiners, agricultural agents and engine-winders; and on women who worked in food production and on the land, and even ones who were simply able to play the piano.

Robert Anderson (Chapter 16) worked as a weaver for most of his life. His short autobiography, published because of his minor songs and poems, tells us plenty about his life as a weaver and provides a fine account of his education in an eighteenth-century charity school. By examining Walter Williamson's replies to the Royal Commission visiting Shetland, we can build up a good picture of what it was like to be a fisherman and crofter in nineteenth-century Shetland. Elsewhere in the same report, ladies from the Shetlands gave similar accounts of what it was like to work professionally as knitters. Like the men, they were tied to producing work for the company store and paid in 'kind' rather than money. We also learn how relatively simple written objects like sheet music, recipe books, diaries, letters and inventories can really flesh out ancestral bones. And we would all love to know the name of a horse owned by an ancestor (Chapter 24) or what became of an ancient family clock (Chapter 26).

The search for ancestral truth will invariably lead to the dark side as well as the light. For those who write down the news there is usually more mileage in the bad and the shocking and this can be of benefit to the family historian. As a result, there is usually little trouble in finding out more about the personalities of family rogues and villains, especially if they were active during the last 150 years or so. In these studies we have thus been presented with detailed pen-pictures of murderers, arsonists, adulterers, bigamists, suicides and incestuous forbearers; skeletons rattle around in cupboards and the terrible question 'Has anyone inherited the related genes?' is asked around the family.

Then there are those ancestors who were simply characters. For some reason, contemporaries (and Victorians in particular) seem to have enjoyed writing copiously about them and have left behind considerable evidence for their often-eccentric doings.

Why do we Become Involved in Family History?

What were my ancestors like? Am I like them? These two key questions go together and the latter, in particular, goes a long way towards explaining why so many of us become involved in genealogy. I think it was the French historian Michelet who noted: 'We are the sum of our ancestors.'

Stephen Close (Chapter 23), a north-country man who enjoys writing for the local newspapers, discovered late in life that he had a poet and writer among his ancestors. The fact that this ancestor was not highly regarded for his literary output seems to be neither here nor there. As Stephen points out today, 'Poet' Close's nineteenth-century writings are much sought after and he is hopeful that he has inherited some of his ancestor's more literary genes.

One of Kelsey Thornton's areas of academic expertise is war poetry, and his fascination with military history was developed in youth through an interest in his grandfather's Boer War experiences. His grandfather came back from the war and later edited newspapers; Kelsey himself is now a much-published author and editor of academic magazines.

I am a musician as well as a writer. My father played guitar and piano in a dance band in the 1930s, whilst his brother had an alto voice (mine is high too!) and made records of classical songs. Their aunt, who was blind, taught the piano for a living (Chapter 4), while my mother's birth mother was a good pianist with a pleasant voice. I was born with music in my blood and music all around me – a very fortunate combination of nature and nurture.

Another interesting, not to say amusing, reason for involvement in genealogy might be the hope of discovering the family's lost wealth. A fellow writer on family history told me that he wished he had a pound for every researcher he met who had family money somewhere 'hidden' or 'locked up' in chancery. If an ancestor had enough money to make a will, then there is some hope (and yes, there is a 'lost money in chancery' tale in our family, too).

Another intriguing point for debate is what we do in the case of the 'non-bloodline relatives' in the family – such as when those involved in family history have been brought up by step-parents. Should there be an interest in looking into their family history as well? The answer lies, perhaps, in the stance taken on the comparative influence of 'nature' and 'nurture' on upbringing and development of personality. There are those who would argue that a step-parent or step-parents have an important influence on the development of personality, and their family tales and history are an important part of family life. The story of a stepmother's involvement in the Gretna

Green Rail Disaster is considered a family tale (Chapter 12), and the recipe book started by Betty Gregson's great-aunt a firm part of family heritage also (Chapter 47).

Research into family also seems to be popular in cases where a fairly recent ancestor died at an early age. If a son, daughter or grandchild of that person is still alive, the catalyst for family history research can be the simple desire to know more about the deceased relative. In such cases, there are usually few family tales on which to hang the hooks of research – just the odd memory here and there. This can make the research all the more challenging and the outcome more rewarding. Such was the case with American Dave Hamm (Chapter 13) who began his work as a result of his grandfather dying when his father was still a teenager. The Shetland bloodline covered in two tales in Chapter 9 and Chapter 13 began life as a distant memory recalled by one who had been 10 years old when her birth mother had died.

Equally interesting are those researchers (mostly married ladies) who have completed their own family trees and are keen to build up a family tree for their children by researching their husband's ancestry as well. Here, research can be as addictive as the quest for blood ancestors, especially when a fascinating character turns up in the tree. Heather Taylor (Chapter 42), Eileen Hopper (Chapter 11) and Eileen Richardson (Chapter 40) have all gone down this line. In Heather's case, a friendship formed with her husband's great-aunt led her to the informative diaries of her husband's relative Joseph Liddell. Eileen Hopper was keen to assist in the cataloguing of important maritime documents passed down through her husband's family. Eileen Richardson managed to trace her husband's ancestry thanks to finding some fairly unusual Christian names. She also discovered that a member of her own family and a member of her husband's family had inhabited the same Victorian tenement and had eventually married – and it was a newly discovered distant cousin living in Canada who provided her with this information.

What are the Key Links between Family History and Other Forms of History?

Family history has, in the past, been regarded as a poor relation of 'real' history. As a trained social historian, I have always disputed this view and it is now time for family historians to stand up and be counted. The tools of the family historian can be extremely useful to the social historian, and the research thus carried out helps in the production of significant microcosms of our varied communities and societies. In other words, tales such as those told in this book form the very framework of our social history.

In addition, used by a teacher in a classroom, family history can become a powerful teaching tool (although it is wise to avoid suggesting that pupils have to research their own trees – this can lead to complications). When workers such as miners, spinners, weavers and sailors appear in a teacher's family, it enables them to talk about real people at work not merely disembodied individuals – and this is helpful to youngsters keen to create visual images. Put ancestral stories together with Victorian diary extracts telling of lost fishing rods, elusive house keys and missed railway trains (Chapter 42) and all human life is there – and eminently recognisable.

The tales told in this book also show how ordinary individuals are necessary to great events and movements. We have one ancestor who was the voice of Disney's Mickey Mouse, a sea captain who flouted the Union navy in the American Civil War, an entrepreneur who organised the first England cricket tour to New Zealand and a nurse called upon to attend on Britain's biggest rail crash. We also have a contributor distantly related to a famous person in song, and others with links to great historical characters like Queen Victoria, Prince Albert,

Lord Palmerston and Napoleon Bonaparte. One ancestor fought at Trafalgar, one at Waterloo, another survived a sniper raid in the Boer War and yet another sat in a tree to gain a clear view of the first massed tank battle in history.

What do these Case Studies Teach Us About Good Practice?

Good practice consists of making sure that as much as possible is written down, catalogued and indexed. Family tales should be jotted down today not left till tomorrow. All family photographs should have notes on the back – in light pencil if necessary. Original primary resources should be sought after where possible and the Internet used with considerable joy and care. Finally, astute family historians ought to be aware of their own mortality. As part of the family, you have a story to tell which, in years to come, will form part of another's ancestry. We all create evidence of some sort relating to our lives. To end on a personal note, I offer some of my own 'evidence' which future Gregson family historians might stumble across without knowing the exact circumstances (see the 'Problems with Sources' section above):

I saw the Beatles from the third row back in a concert at the Lonsdale Cinema in Carlisle in 1963. I have a related newspaper cutting, which mentions my name.

I was involved with a pop group in a church hall on the night Kennedy died in 1963. The hall emptied within seconds of the news. I have memories of that night and what we all thought of the American president at the time.

I saw Neil Armstrong land on the moon while watching a television in a shop window on the Italian Riviera in 1969 and still have the relevant diary entry.

I was in Trafalgar Square the night England won the Football World Cup in 1966 and sent a postcard home to my parents after bumping into the legendary Portuguese footballer Eusebio. We still have the card.

Above all, as an undergraduate, I drew lots to be in the second row from the front when Martin Luther King was presented with a Doctorate of Civil Law at Newcastle University in 1968. I have vivid memories of this remarkable man.

My own notes on these events may be of interest and use to a social historian writing about life in late twentieth-century Britain, or they may not. They will certainly be there for any descendants to read or disregard as they choose. As the studies in this book show, all it takes is a snippet of information to set the trail for new discoveries.